TWAYNE'S WORLD AUTHORS SERIES

A Survey of the World's Literature

Sylvia E. Bowman, Indiana University

GENERAL EDITOR

SPAIN

Gerald Wade, Vanderbilt University

Janet W. Díaz, University of North Carolina at Chapel Hill

EDITORS

Vicente Espinel

TWAS 440

Supposed Likeness of Vicente Espinel
From the original in the possession of the Diputación Provincial de
Málaga.

VICENTE ESPINEL

A. ANTONY HEATHCOTE

University of Sheffield

TWAYNE PUBLISHERS

A DIVISION OF G. K. HALL & CO., BOSTON

Library of Congress Cataloging in Publication Data

Heathcote, A. Antony
  Vicente Espinel.

  (Twayne's world authors series ; TWAS 440 :   Spain)
  Bibliography: p. 155–57.
  Includes index.
  1. Espinel, Vicente, 1550?–1624.   2. Authors,
Spanish—17th century—Biography.
PQ6390.E56Z68   868'.3'09 [B]   76-53560
ISBN 0-8057-6169-1

To June

Contents

About the Author

Antony Heathcote is a graduate in modern languages of the University of Manchester where he also pursued postgraduate research in Golden Age drama, concentrating principally on Tirso de Molina and Mira de Amescua. After a period of service as an Education Officer in the R.A.F., he was appointed to his present post in the Department of Hispanic Studies of the University of Sheffield. His work in teaching and research has been mainly in the field of the novel and the theatre of the Golden Age. In 1968/69, he was Visiting Associate Professor in McGill University and was responsible for setting up an M.A. Graduate Program in which he taught and directed research in Spanish literature of the sixteenth and seventeenth centuries. Antony Heathcote has published articles and reviews on a number of Golden Age figures, most frequently Tirso de Molina and Calderón.

Preface

Major studies of Espinel's work as a poet and novelist have been few for one who enjoyed such a high reputation in his day and whose *Marcos de Obregón* is recognized as a classic of seventeenth-century prose. One or two of his poems have found their way into anthologies, but his verse miscellany, *Diversas rimas*, had to wait 365 years before it saw a second edition, and only three unabridged editions of *Marcos de Obregón* have been published in this century, the last, edited by María Soledad Carrasco Urgoiti, in 1972. Most of the work done on Espinel as a poet and musician is in the form of articles in learned journals, as is the criticism of aspects of *Marcos de Obregón*, with the notable exception of Haley's masterly study. An attempt has been made in this book to review these contributions to our understanding of Espinel's life and work and offer some fresh ideas and opinions.

The first section of the book seeks to present the facts of the author's life and assess his reputation among his contemporaries, trimming from his life story some of the fanciful elements incorporated as a result of Espinel's prose and poetry being used uncritically as a source of biographical data. In the ensuing pages, both Espinel's verse miscellany and his autobiographical novel are placed within the context of the literature of the day, and the relationship between his work and its ideological background evaluated, particularly as projections of Espinel's personality and habits of style. Each work is critically analyzed and its salient features thrown into relief.

In Chapter 2, *Diversas rimas* is studied as a structured collection of poems, with special emphasis given to Espinel's versification, his main preoccupations and themes, and to certain features of his poetic style in order to gauge his place among the galaxy of talents in the Golden Age. Certain aspects of *Marcos de Obregón* are isolated in Chapter 3 in order to clarify the book's debt to other types of novel popular at the time, especially the picaresque, and to try to explain what contributes to make it a unique blend of fact and fiction, past and present, episode and digression. Thus prepared, the reader can then proceed to the final chapter where he will find a detailed analysis of *Marcos de Obregón*, which lays particular stress upon the presentation of the Squire as Espinel's *alter ego,* the author's use of the flashback technique to move from one time-level to another and the book's wide-ranging geography.

It is hoped that, as a result of this study of Espinel's life and work, the early *Diversas rimas* and the late *Marcos de Obregón* may be seen as somehow complementing each other stylistically and thematically. Espinel's talent for description, particularly of Nature in her varying moods, his love of music, his eye for color and significant detail can all be seen in both works; a taste for antithesis, revealed in *Diversas rimas* and projected into the novel, is matched by a counterbalancing dislike of pedantry and excess, and a preference for directness and clarity. In terms of theme, the verse miscellany and *Marcos de Obregón* have a "confessional" aspect in which the author adopts another *persona* to purge himself of the excesses of his temperament and early conduct, seeking to achieve that fortitude and stoicism which is expressed in the Spanish word, *paciencia* (patience, in the context of perseverance).

The translations from Espinel's poetry and prose are mine since *Diversas rimas* has not been rendered into English and the early nineteenth-century version of *Marcos de Obregón* by Major Algernon Langton was not available to me at the time this book was written.

I would like to express my sincere gratitude to the Spanish Co-Editor of this series, Gerald E. Wade, for his tolerance and friendly advice. My thanks also go to the University of Sheffield for a period of leave which has allowed me to finish this much-delayed project.

A. ANTONY HEATHCOTE

University of Sheffield

Chronology

1550   December 28, Vicente Espinel is baptized in the Church of Santa Cecilia in Ronda.

1570–   Espinel is enrolled in the Faculty of Arts of the University of
1572   Salamanca where he studies for two sessions.

1572   A chaplaincy is established in Ronda by Espinel's aunt and uncle. Espinel is to be its first incumbent.

1578(?) Probable visit to Seville. Composition of "Sátira contra las damas de Sevilla" ("Satire on the Ladies of Seville").

1581–   Visit to Italy in the entourage of the Duke of Medina-
1584(?) Sidonia. Joins in literary and musical life of Milan and, soon after arrival, writes verses for the Cathedral in memory of Ana de Austria.

1585–   Studies for the priesthood in Málaga and obtains the support
1586   of the Bishop, Francisco Pacheco.

1586   September, competes unsuccessfully for a benefice in the Church of Santa María la Mayor in Ronda.

1587   Secures a half-benefice in the same church. Report of competition praises his command of Latin and his musicianship.

1587   Visits Madrid where Alonso de Ercilla writes *aprobación* (approval) for a volume of verse later to become Espinel's *Diversas rimas (Miscellaneous Verse).*

1587–   Ronda poems, written at this time, show him unhappy amid
1590   the petty provincialism of his home town and seeking a new patron following the appointment of Bishop Pacheco to Cordova.

1590   In Granada, where he witnesses and records in verse the explosion of a powder magazine.

1591   *Diversas rimas (Miscellaneous Verse)* published in Madrid. Appointed to a chaplaincy in Ronda; names a substitute and remains in the capital.

1594   Ronda authorities protest at Espinel's absenteeism. Ordered to return. Medical evidence of gout secures temporary stay of this order.

1597–   Renewal of complaints to the King concerning Espinel's fail-
1598   ure to fulfil his duties and other excesses. Tried by Church authorities; fined and warned.

1599   Appointed chapel-master at the Chapel of the Bishop of Plasencia in the Church of San Andrés in Madrid, a post he occupies for the rest of his life.

1603   Business trip to Valladolid, then temporary capital.

1604   Transfer of power of attorney to handle his Ronda affairs.

1605   Represents Madrid clerics in negotiation with tax officials. Another trip to Valladolid.

1609   Begins work as a book censor for the Inquisition, a post he retains until his death, issuing a steady stream of *aprobaciones*. Member of leading literary academies.

1612   Gives evidence before the commission investigating the life and miracles of Saint Isidore, prior to canonization.

1614   Submits Latin hymn in a poetic competition in honor of the beatification of Saint Teresa.

1615   Listed by Cristóbal Suárez de Figueroa as one of the leading musicians of the period; named by Gonzalo de Céspedes y Meneses as inventor of the strophe known as the *espinela*.

1616   Contributes a Latin epigram to the competition celebrating the installation of a statue of the Virgin Mary in the Cathedral of Toledo.

1618   *Relaciones de la vida del Escudero Marcos de Obregón (Account of the Life of the Squire Marcos de Obregón)* published in Madrid.

1620   Submits a sonnet for the poetic competition in honor of the beatification of Saint Isidore.

1623   Promoted to senior chaplain. Writes his last *aprobación*.

1624   February 4, dies in the Capilla del Obispo and is buried in the Church of San Andrés.

CHAPTER 1

Life and Times

I Introduction

ACCOUNTS of Vicente Espinel's life have often been colored by excessive reliance on the fictionalized autobiography contained in his major work, *Relaciones de la vida del Escudero Marcos de Obregón (Account of the Life of the Squire Marcos de Obregón)*,[1] published in Madrid in 1618, and, to a lesser degree, in his *Diversas rimas (Miscellaneous Verse)*[2] of 1591. Only in the last twenty years have attempts been made to produce a documented biography so that the special relationship between art and life, fiction and fact in his novel has begun to emerge.[3] It is important to establish the known facts of Espinel's career — few though they may be — so that a proper assessment may be made of the existing literary material wherein the milestones of a lifetime, recollected and transformed in the tranquility of old age, are combined with fictional episodes, moral commentary, and observations on a variety of topics to produce a book of memoirs which is intended to serve the twin Horatian aims of entertainment and moral uplift. An essential part of this creative process is the way in which the author produces an *alter ego* in his hero Marcos and then sets up an elaborate system of cross-references between himself and the Squire, between the past and the present. Although this technique is not exploited to the full by Espinel, it is easy to see in it an exploration of the possibilities of the novel as an instrument for examining the complicated relationship between art and life.

It is not only Espinel's own work which has contributed to the myths surrounding his life. He enjoyed a reputation as a poet and musician during his lifetime which was based not so much on his published output as upon his influence on a wide circle of the literary lions of the day. He enjoyed the respect and friendship of Cervantes, Lope de Vega, Mateo Alemán, Francisco de Quevedo, and

13

many other leading figures. Well-known Church dignitaries such as
the Cardinal Archbishop of Toledo and Dr. Cetina, the Vicar of
Madrid, gave him their favor and protection, and his work as official
book censor brought him into contact with major authors of the day.
Two tangible results of this image-building process were that Espinel was credited with the invention of a verse-form, the *espinela*,
and with the addition of the fifth string to the Spanish guitar. As we
shall see later, modern research has shown that, although Espinel
was responsible for the popularization of these two artistic innovations, he did not in fact invent them.

II *Birth and Family*

Vicente Espinel was born of a family of modest means in Ronda in
southern Spain toward the end of December, 1550. The exact date
of birth is not known, but a composite version of his baptismal
certificate shows that he was christened on December 28 of that
year. The surname Espinel, which does not appear on the record,
may have been adopted from his mother's side of the family, a fairly
common practice at the time, although in a recently discovered
document dating from toward the end of Espinel's life, the author
gives his father's name as Francisco Gómez Espinel. According to
the evidence of the "Canción a su patria" ("Song to His Homeland")
in the *Diversas rimas (Miscellaneous Verse)* the family came originally from the mountains of northern Spain and was involved in the
Reconquest and, more specifically, in the capture of Ronda from the
Moors in 1485. In return for their services, Espinel's ancestors were
given land in the Ronda area by the Catholic Monarchs. Another
poem in the collection, "Elegía a la muerte de su madre" ("Elegy on
the Death of His Mother"), also tells us that there were other children besides Vicente, but only a nephew, Jacinto de Espinel
Adorno, author of a pastoral novel, has left any mark upon literary
history.

III *Education*

The period between his birth (1550) and 1570, the year of his
entrance to the University of Salamanca, is not documented. We are
entitled to assume that he received the normal education of a
bourgeois lad from the provinces — a grounding in grammar and
rhetoric and in his case, presumably, instruction in music. His

teacher was quite probably the same Juan Cansino mentioned in *Marcos de Obregón* (I, 142),[4] whose family did live in Ronda at the time.

Espinel describes himself in the "Canción a su patria" as setting out for Salamanca: "Tender, naked and poor"(72).[5] It is perhaps necessary to point out, however, that although Espinel's parents may not have been well-off, his aunt and uncle had the means to establish a chaplaincy for their nephew on his return from Salamanca in 1572, and documents show that he administered the property upon which this benefice was founded for the rest of his life.

Espinel's name appears on the register of students in the Faculty of Arts of the University of Salamanca for two sessions, beginning in 1570. It may be assumed that he pursued the normal Arts course of the time consisting of the study of grammar, rhetoric, and Classical authors. If the corresponding section of *Marcos de Obregón* is, indeed, autobiographical, it would seem that Espinel gave private music lessons to earn extra money and that his pleasant manner brought him the friendship of the Corregidor of Salamanca. There are also references in the book to prominent academics teaching in Salamanca during this period, such as Father Mancio, Dr. Medina, and Francisco de Salinas. It was to the latter that Fray Luis de León dedicated his ode "El aire se serena" ("The air grows still"), and the mention of the name of that distinguished musician here and in the long poem "La casa de la Memoria" ("The House of Memory") strengthens the belief that Espinel undertook some formal study of music at this time. Certainly he attended performances by Salinas and Juan de Navarro and musical soirées at the house of Agustina de Torres. It was a decisive period in his musical development, and the impact of this intellectual experience was to remain with him long afterward.

Student riots in connection with the imprisonment of Fray Luis de León by the Inquisition brought about the closure of the University in 1572, and Espinel returned home in that year. His experiences en route obviously contributed to the liveliness of his description of picaresque encounters and adventures on the road to Ronda.

IV   1572–81

There is no record outside his literary work of Espinel's activities in this period. Attempts to fill the gap on the basis of conjecture, the evidence of the novel, and the suggestions of the poems illustrate some of the difficulties which beset the biographer of Espinel.

Claims have been made that the author returned to Salamanca in 1572, shortly after taking possession of a family chaplaincy in Ronda. In the same year, however, he is supposed to have been in Madrid acting as tutor to the young Lope de Vega. Two years later he is said to have gone to Santander to join the ill-fated fleet of Pedro Meléndez de Avilés which was struck by pestilence before it left port. Subsequently Espinel may have spent four years in Valladolid in the service of the Count of Lemos before moving on to Seville where he associated with the cultural circles frequented by the painter Francisco de Pacheco, the poets Fernando de Herrera and Luis Barahona de Soto, and the organist Francisco de Peraza. It was at this time that he wrote his "Sátira contra las damas de Sevilla" ("Satire on the Ladies of Seville") which earned him a certain notoriety in literary and society circles.[6] It has also been affirmed that he first met Ottavio Gonzaga, whose friendship and protection he later enjoyed in Italy, at the Siege of Maestricht in 1579. On the way to Italy, Espinel is thought to have been captured by the Turks and to have spent a short period of captivity in Algiers.

External evidence to support these assertions, mainly based on passages in *Marcos de Obregón*, is unfortunately lacking. For instance, during the second visit to Salamanca, it has been claimed that Espinel studied at the Colegio Mayor de San Pelayo. His name does not appear on college or university lists for the period concerned, and it seems possible that, despite his academic pretensions, Espinel left Salamanca without graduating. Documents relating to a later application for a benefice note that he failed to produce proof of attendance at San Pelayo. As for the special relationship between Lope de Vega and Espinel, it is tempting to imagine the youthful Lope sitting at the feet of the "Master", Vicente Espinel, but once again the evidence is suspect, based simply on fulsome praise of Espinel contained in Lope's occasional verse and not necessarily to be taken literally. The Santander episode, however, as described in *Marcos de Obregón*, does have an eye-witness quality and a wealth of circumstantial detail which suggest that Marcos' experience may coincide with Espinel's own, but here again, the biographer is hampered by lack of external evidence. The same constraints apply to Espinel's supposed service with the Count of Lemos. Marcos' account includes references to events and people which lend credence to the transfer of experience from the protagonist to the creator. The praise of the Castros also causes one to believe that Espinel knew them and relied on them for patronage, but once again, documentary evidence to support the hypothesis is lacking.

The period spent in Seville is perhaps in a different category. Cervantes amusingly relates how "a famous poet of today" wrote a satire on society ladies and was upbraided by one of them for leaving her out.[7] The reference seems to be to Espinel's earliest known work, the "Sátira contra las damas de Sevilla" ("Satire on the Ladies of Seville"), a work which is surely too well observed to be based on hearsay. The references in *Marcos de Obregón* to the columns in the Alameda and to local gentry reinforce this view, as does the naming, in "La casa de la Memoria", of the artistic coterie to which he may have temporarily belonged. It was from Seville also that he would have set sail for Italy, following the plague outbreak in 1581. The excursion to Flanders, where Espinel is supposed to have met Ottavio Gonzaga, is less credible, since there is no independent evidence of such a visit and Gonzaga returned to Spain in the year Espinel allegedly set sail for Italy. It is likely that the two men met for the first time in Milan.

As for Marcos' capture by Turkish pirates and subsequent captivity in Algiers, Espinel's sources are clearly literary. The circumstances of the seizure recall an episode in Gil Polo's pastoral novel, *La Diana enamorada (Diana in Love)*, and the story of Marcos' servitude owes more to travellers' tales, to Cervantes, and to other writers of so-called "Moorish novels" than to lived experience.[8] It was customary for novels of adventure of the day to include such episodes, with their sentimentalized, stereotyped portrayal of the Moors, their stock situations, and their religious propaganda, and nothing in the *Marcos de Obregón* suggests anything other than a literary source. It is perhaps worth pointing out that there is no external record of Espinel's captivity nor do any of his contemporaries, literary or ecclesiastical, refer to what should have been a noteworthy event in the author's life.

V *Italy*

Espinel's stay in Italy is well attested. He arrived in Milan in the advance party of the Duke of Medina-Sidonia in 1581 and was soon commissioned to provide elegiac verses and mottoes in Spanish and Latin to decorate the cathedral as part of a service to the memory of

Ana de Austria.[9] Espinel enjoyed the protection of Ottavio Gonzaga and seems to have benefited from contacts with the literary and musical circle attached to the house of Antonio de Londoño. In his will, the author remembers a debt owed to a Milanese merchant dating from this period of his life. Although troubled by the humidity of northern Italy — a fact which may have been partly responsible for his return to Spain — Espinel clearly profited in terms of cultural development and prestige from his trip.

His literary activities seem to resume about mid-1584, in Madrid, with the widening of his circle of artistic acquaintances and the consolidating of his reputation as a poet and musician.

VI   Return to Ronda

Espinel returned to his home town in 1586. The pleasure of his homecoming was, however, short-lived. His mother — to whom he seems to have been especially attached — had recently died, and his first efforts to obtain advancement in the Church failed because of his "little voice." He took up a half-benefice in 1587, and four years later, thanks to the continuing patronage of the Bishop of Málaga, he gained the post of chaplain to the Hospital Real de Santa Bárbara. The attractions of the capital — the lionizing, the commissions, the friendship of the great, the favor and protection — were, in Espinel's case, to be set against the lack of recognition, the envy, the backbiting and provincialism of Ronda. It is small wonder that he, like many priest-writers of the day, fell foul of the municipal and ecclesiastical authorities for absenteeism. His change of attitude toward the place of his birth is remarkably well illustrated in *Diversas rimas (Miscellaneous Verse)* by the "Canción a su patria" ("Song to His Homeland") and the poem addressed to the Bishop of Málaga.[10] In the first, Ronda is the "dear homeland," "my city," the "beloved country" embracing its lost son and offering him "Health, peace and happiness" after his wanderings; in the second, Ronda's crags are a prison in which Espinel finds himself oppressed by envy.

The fourteen years which followed Espinel's return to Ronda tell a story of constant bickering as he tried to better himself in the Church and keep up his artistic contacts in the capital. The attempt to lead a double life as a priest in Ronda and a poet and musician in Madrid inevitably led to disaster. It is clear from the Ronda poems in *Diversas rimas* that, after the champagne days of Italy and Madrid, Espinel soon found the pettiness of his home town stifling and began to seek relief and escape. Visits to Granada may have given him the title of *bachiller en artes* and the opportunity to describe in verse the explosion and fire of February, 1590. Once his protector, the Bishop of Málaga, had gone to Cordova, Espinel constantly sought escape to Madrid. He was beset by gout and depressed by the lack of appreciation from the people of Ronda. His literary friends were in the capital where he was sought after and admired. Once appointed to the Santa Bárbara chaplaincy, he lost no time in following common practice at the time by naming a substitute so that he might remain in Madrid and enjoy the fruits of a literary reputation enhanced by the recent publication of his verse miscellany, *Diversas rimas*.

In 1594, the authorities in Ronda petitioned the King for their chaplain's return. Espinel managed to obtain a postponement on the grounds of ill health but was finally compelled to go back and attend to the spiritual needs of the poor of the Hospital Real. That he did not do so conscientiously is attested by a further complaint against him in October, 1597 in which he is accused of living well on his stipend without doing anything to earn it. To this charge of dereliction of duty was later added the more sinister one of profligacy. Espinel was tried by the ecclesiastical authorities and fined. By mid-1598 he seems to have learned his lesson and to be applying himself diligently to looking after his flock. At last, in 1599, came the long-awaited chance to establish himself in Madrid and thus a new chapter opens in Espinel's life.

VII   Diversas rimas (Miscellaneous Verse)

This collection of poems reflects the dichotomy in Espinel's life as a priest-poet up to the late 1580's, and the circumstances surrounding its publication in 1591 help us to understand the difficulties he faced in trying to earn his living as a priest in Ronda while, at the same time, maintaining his contacts and reputation in Madrid. In a later chapter we shall analyze the book in some detail. It is sufficient at the moment to situate the work within the Ronda period before moving on to Espinel's experiences in Madrid.

It appears that, immediately before securing the half-benefice at Santa María la Mayor, Espinel was in Madrid putting the finishing touches to his manuscript of *Diversas rimas (Miscellaneous Verse)*, for which Alonso de Ercilla wrote an approval in 1587. Threatened by the loss of his patron Bishop Pacheco, Espinel also had to look for a new source of patronage. The Duke of Alba's steward, Luis de Castilla and the Marquis of Peñafiel were both addressed in verse until eventually *Miscellaneous Verse* was published under the patronage of the Duke of Alba. In the meantime Espinel was also gathering laudatory verses from literary friends such as Lope de Vega and Lupercio Leonardo de Argensola and other persons of influence such as Hernando de Soto and Félix Arias Girón.

It is clear from the list of panegyrists that Espinel's interests are centered in Madrid. The miscellany itself mirrors not only his feelings as a young man setting out from Ronda to make his way in the world but also his attempts to win favor with patrons, his literary friendships, and his later annoyance at feeling himself imprisoned in Ronda. The poems tell of his inner life and of external events which helped to shape his career to date; they offer a valuable review of highlights of his life up to the late 1580's and, as such, they complement the prose account contained in *Marcos de Obregón*.

The dangers of an over-literal interpretation of these verses, however, are best illustrated by the references to Célida in the love poems. Célida has been taken to be the poetic pseudonym of Antonia Maldonado y Calatayud on the basis of a single mention of the lady's name in *Marcos de Obregón*. It is possible to build up a story of unrequited passion from the poems in which Espinel's advances are rejected in favor of a more attractive suitor whom Célida later marries. This rejection, the story goes, causes Espinel to abandon Seville and begin his travels.[11] The external evidence for such a romantic episode is, however, minimal, and we would do well to bear in mind the words of Don Quixote when he reminds us of the gulf which separates the reality and the fiction of a poet's Phyllis, Amaryllis, Laura etc: "Do you think that the Amarillyses, the Phyllises, the Sylvias, the Dianas, the Galateas, the Alidas and other such, of which the novels and ballads are full, were really ladies of flesh and blood and belonged to those who praise or praised them? Of course not, but rather do they invent the majority of them to act as object of their poetry . . ." (*DQ*, II, 274–75).

VIII   *Madrid*

And so, in 1599, Espinel escaped from the uncongenial atmosphere of Ronda and took up an appointment as chapel-master of the Capilla del Obispo de Plasencia attached to the Church of San Andrés in Madrid. About this time, too, he began to assume the titles of *Maestro* (Master) and *Licenciado* (Licenciate). There has been much critical speculation about this matter. The first title may simply be an honorary one associated with his work as choirmaster and church musician, but the second is an academic title which he is assumed to have gained at the University of Alcalá. The records of that institution for the period concerned, however, do not show him as being registered for the degree. As in the case of the title of *Bachiller* (Bachelor), which he also used, it seems that neither Espinel nor subsequent researchers have been able to supply documentary proof of his claims. Nevertheless, his works contain evidence that Espinel's reputation for erudition was well deserved. Lack of external evidence does not invalidate his claim to having been regarded as an authority in his day on matters of literary and musical taste.

His new appointment was the start of a long period of activity as a musician and man of letters. The choral and instrumental music performed in the Capilla del Obispo was Espinel's responsibility. He trained the choir, chose and arranged suitable pieces for performance, and composed original works. His poems appeared in the *Romancero General (General Anthology of Ballads)*[12] and other collections, and he wrote prefatory verses and epigrams for works by Alemán, Quevedo, and many others. His name is listed among those attending meetings of literary groups, such as the Academia de Madrid, and he was one of the first members, along with Cervantes and Lope, of the brotherhood of authors which, under the protection of the Duke of Lerma, was founded in 1608 and called itself the Congregación de Esclavos del Santísimo Sacramento. This coterie later included Salas Barbadillo, Quevedo, and Calderón and obviously constituted an influential group on the Madrid literary scene. It is a pity we know so little about its aims and activities, but for Espinel to belong to it is an indication of significant status in the literary community.[13] The frustrating years in Ronda had been put behind him; he had renewed his literary contacts and was enjoying a reputation as an accomplished musician, an elegant versifier, and a respected literary theorist. He now had a tidy income, a house in Madrid, and a post which offered him not only the opportunity to exercise his musical talents but also the leisure to pursue his literary activities. He appointed a nominee to manage his affairs in Ronda, and, although he did not relinquish his benefices there, he never returned thereafter to the place of his birth.

From a sonnet published for the first time by Haley,[14] it is clear that Espinel joined the chorus of protest against Philip III's decision to move the Court in 1601 from Madrid to Valladolid. It is an ironic sonnet whose sting is in the tail. After listing the abuses which resulted from the move and the disreputable sections of the community who were profiting from it, Espinel concludes: "For this and other reasons this move is just." The literature of the day echoed Espinel's sentiments, comparing Valladolid to a latter-day Babylon. The temporary capital was hopelessly overcrowded, and corruption was rife as the hangers-on, prostitutes, dealers, petty officials and property owners swarmed round the Court set, hoping to make a quick profit.

Espinel's work kept him in Madrid for most of the period up to 1601 when the Court returned there. For one thing, he had to keep an eye on the administration of his ecclesiastical and property interests in Ronda. A document of 1604 shows that he transferred his power of attorney from Andrés López de Peralta to Lucas Gómez del Valle. He also acted as witness to the property transactions of his parishioners in Madrid and, in 1605, was called upon by fellow-clerics to represent the Cabildo de la Clerecía in negotiations with the tax authorities. This sign of confidence contrasts with the earlier hostility and distrust felt by his ecclesiastical colleagues in Ronda and with the charges of negligence formerly leveled against him. The truth is that, from 1599, Espinel was doing what he wanted to do, combining his Church duties with his passion for music and literature. He felt able to become involved in the affairs of the community in a way which was never possible for him in Ronda.

There is evidence that Espinel left Madrid to visit Valladolid on two occasions while the Court was there. The first was probably a business trip made in 1603 and the second, in 1605, was in connection with representations of the Madrid clerics to the tax authorities. During the second of these visits, Espinel seems to have found time for literary activity, since he wrote prefatory verses to the *Historia Euangelica (Evangelical History)* of Juan de Arce Solórzano and to another work by Simón de Villalobos y Benavides. Espinel's poems were also included in two anthologies published in Valladolid in 1605 — Pedro de Espinosa's *Flores de poetas ilustres (Gems of Famous Poets)* and the *Segunda parte del Romancero General (Second Part of the General Anthology of Ballads)* compiled by Miguel de Madrigal. This evidence of broader literary activity strengthens the case for believing that the poet also renewed contact with Madrid exiles by attending sessions of the group known as the Academia de Valladolid.

Espinel was based in Madrid, however, for the rest of his life. The period beginning with his acceptance of the post of chapel-master and ending with his death seems to have been a happy and productive one in which Espinel enjoyed the confidence of the authorities and the respect of fellow-writers and -musicians. His portly figure was seen in all the best circles, and he became more relaxed, putting behind him the reputation for harshness and irascibility which stemmed from his Ronda days. Only his poor health and the frequent attacks of gout, which troubled him during most of his adult life, soured this phase of his career. Even that, however, had its profitable side because, although he might no longer be able to play the *vihuela*, that early form of the guitar on which he was formerly so proficient, the evidence is that he used the long periods of confinement to his quarters profitably, working as a book censor, writing poetry and preparing the draft of his great work, *Marcos de Obregón*.

IX *Book Censorship*

The Vicar of Madrid displayed confidence in Espinel's literary judgment by recommending his appointment as book censor for the Inquisition. The exact date of the appointment is not known but Espinel's earliest known *aprobación* dates from the beginning of 1609. Thenceforth, he gave official approval to a stream of books, and he remained in the position until his death.[15] The post, allied to his other literary and musical activities, seems to have led to his being cultivated in Madrid literary circles. Quevedo's *Buscón (The Sharper)* has one of the minor characters priding himself on having dined "more than a few times with Espinel,"[16] and Miguel Botello lists him as a member of Madrid's new Parnassus. Certainly he is known to have been a member of several literary coteries of the day. In addition to his membership of the Academia de Madrid and the Congregación de Esclavos del Santísimo Sacramento, Espinel also seems to have been associated with the Academia Selvaje and the Academia de Saldaña. He contributed dedicatory verses to a number of works and took part in literary competitions such as the ones held in honor of the beatification of Saint Teresa and Saint Isidore. He enjoyed a reputation as a "great censor," and from early in 1609 until the year before his death, *aprobaciones* and *censuras* by him appear as part of the preliminaries of a wide range of works in prose and verse. Historical accounts, devotional poetry, mythological works, collections of plays, pastoral and picaresque fiction — all these genres and more were subjected to Espinel's scrutiny.

Espinel's censorship of contemporary literature helps to explain, at least in part, the high esteem in which he was held by his peers. Although he himself wrote comparatively little, his influence is clear from the deferential way he is referred to by other authors. He is considered to be a model of literary elegance and an arbiter of taste. Setting aside the conventional phrases in his *aprobaciones*, it is possible to deduce that part of this reputation for elegance and discrimination stems from Espinel's admiration for the Horatian concept of combining pleasure with instruction in literature. Other elements in his literary theory are the Aristotelian principle of clearly defining the universal concerns of the poet as distinct from the particular concerns of the historian and also his insistence, in line with Renaissance literary theory, that episodes in a narrative should not be digressive but form part of a homogeneous action, "very uniform in all its parts".[17] Espinel's standards as a censor, based upon the traditional views of the Inquisition and reinforced by his intimate knowledge of Classical and Renaissance literary theory, are perhaps best defined in a passage of the *Marcos de Obregón* in which the protagonist discusses with a hermit the question of the responsibilities of authorship:

Books for publication should be the bearers of doctrine and pleasure to teach and delight . . . Books for publication should contain great purity and chasteness of language; purity in the choice of words and in the appropriateness of concepts and chasteness in not introducing irrelevances that do not legitimately fit the subject matter. . . . (II, 17–18)

Whether or not Espinel, in his own work, managed to achieve the high standards he set for others or whether, indeed, those works which carried the seal of his approval themselves conformed to the standards he ascribed to them is not at issue. What is certain is that the name of Espinel was associated with these literary ideals. During his censorship, Espinel was a shadowy but influential figure on the literary scene, a model for all to follow and, in his later years, he was considered an elder statesman of Spanish letters to be respect-fully listened to and deferred to as he presided over the Muses.

X *Lope de Vega*

Although Lope's effusive praise of Espinel in his *Laurel de Apolo (Laurels of Apollo)* and elsewhere has led to probably unjustified speculation about the pupil-master relationship between the two men, it is nevertheless clear that there was a special bond between them.[18] Espinel wrote *aprobaciones* for several volumes of Lope's collected plays as well as for other works, and references to Espinel by Lope are always warm and admiring of his talents as a musician and a poet, talents which Lope felt had not received their due acknowledgement and reward. One such reference which is of spe-cial interest is made by Lope in a letter to the Duke of Sessa. Trying, in 1617, to enlist the support of the Duke for Espinel, Lope describes him as: "a man outstanding in Castilian and Latin verse, apart from his uniqueness in music; and his character can no longer be harsh, for even the one that has been superlatively so is tem-pered with time or lessened by frailty."[19]

The reputation for harshness of character — presumably a throwback to his Ronda days and his battles with authority — may have died hard, but there can be no doubt about the professional esteem which Espinel enjoyed among his fellow-writers during the period from 1609 until ill health curtailed his literary activities around 1622. A mark of Lope's special esteem is given by the dedi-cation to Espinel of the *Caballero de Illescas (The Gentleman of Illescas)* which is included in the *Parte catorze (Part Fourteen)* of his collected plays. In the preliminaries to the play Lope refers to his "Master" as "Apollo of Latin and Spanish Poetry," the "outstanding giant of the musical arts" and acknowledges his own debt to a talent not sufficiently recognized. On other occasions Lope calls Espinel "a great talent of our age" and says he was honored as "a unique Latin and Spanish poet of that time."

XI Marcos de Obregón

Espinel's major work, *Relaciones de la vida del Escudero Marcos de Obregón (Account of the Life of the Squire Marcos de Obregón)* was published in Madrid in 1618. It is noticeable that during the period 1614–16 there is a decline in Espinel's literary activity. Apart from a few *aprobaciones*, little is heard of him. It may be that for long spells he fell victim to his old enemy gout. But he was not idle. During this period he must have composed the volume of pseudo-memoirs which has been chiefly responsible for his place in literary history.

By late 1616 he was in Toledo looking for a patron for his work. The Archbishop of Toledo, Cardinal Bernardo de Sandoval y Rojas, was a suitable candidate, a well-known Maecenas to whom Tirso, Cervantes, Lope, Quevedo, Góngora, and Valdivielso had cause to be grateful for his interest, protection, and hospitality. The approach to the Archbishop may have been made through one of several intermediaries mentioned in *Marcos de Obregón*: the famous preacher Fray Hortensio Félix Paravicino who was on an assignment in Toledo in connection with the consecration of the sanctuary of the Cathedral; José de Valdivielso, chaplain of the Mozarabic chapel; the Oviedo brothers who were members of the Archbishop's staff. The Archbishop was obviously sympathetic to the appeal for favor since Espinel recognized the award of a pension by dedicating his book to him. According to Salas Barbadillo, the pension was intended to enable Espinel to spend his old age more comfortably.

The work itself, which constituted a most original attempt to combine autobiography and fiction, must have enhanced Espinel's career at a time when, after nearly twenty years in the capital, he might have lapsed into relative obscurity. One can judge its early success by the fact that three editions appeared in 1618, and in the same year, a translation of the first part was published in Paris.[20] Curiously, however, his contemporaries made few references to it, failing to recognize its originality.

XII *Death*

During the last three years of his life, Espinel's literary activities were confined to book censorship. At San Andrés, he was appointed to the post of senior chaplain, but the gout to which he often referred in *Miscellaneous Verse* and *Marcos de Obregón* and for which he had been receiving treatment from the age of about thirty-four, finally reduced him to almost complete immobility. He dictated his will on February 1, 1624 and was unable to sign it himself because he had lost the use of his right hand. The document is conventional save that Espinel surprisingly remembers a forty-three-year-old debt of twenty ducats to a merchant in Milan. He directed that his outstanding debts be paid or that masses be said for those of his creditors who were dead. His books were to be sold for requiem masses. The only relative mentioned in the will was his nephew, Jacinto, who was to receive the family chaplaincy in Ronda.

Vicente Espinel died on February 4, 1624, at the age of seventy-three, in the Capilla del Obispo where he had served for nearly a quarter of a century. He was buried in the Church of San Andrés.

XIII   *Reputation as a Musician*

References by Lope de Vega, Cervantes, and other contemporaries have helped to perpetuate the myth that Espinel added a fifth string to the "Spanish" guitar.[21] In the *Dorotea*, for example, in a passage which puts the date of its introduction at 1587, Lope exclaims: "May God forgive Vicente Espinel who brought us . . . the five strings of the guitar, with which the noble instruments are now being forgotten."[22] The pioneer method for the "new" instrument, Dr. Juan Carlos Amat's *Guitarra española de cinco órdenes (Five-Course Spanish Guitar)*, published in 1596, does not mention Espinel's supposed contribution. The reference to a meeting with him and to his addition of the fifth string, in a later treatise by Nicolás Doizi de Velasco, seems to have been the one which, along with the assertions of fellow-writers, has been echoed through the years. A recent biographer of Espinel still alludes to his "invention."[23]

Research by literary critics and musicologists has shown that the five-string compromise between the popular instrument and the aristocratic *vihuela*, with its six or seven courses, was in existence before Espinel was born.[24] Juan Bermudo includes it in his *Declaración de instrumentos (Register of Instruments)* of 1549, and Miguel de Fuenllana was writing for the five-stringed guitar by the mid-1550's. The second half of the century saw the decline of the *vihuela*, the aristocratic solo instrument principally used for the performance of contrapuntal music. An accommodation was reached between the *vihuela* and the popular four-stringed guitar, not so much by adding a string to the latter as by suppressing the top string of the aristocratic instrument. This "new" guitar enjoyed a European vogue in the seventeenth century as a virtuoso instrument, ideal for salon entertainment.

Having taken away from Espinel the honor, as it were, of inventing the instrument, we should not underestimate his role in popularizing it. Cristóbal Suárez de Figueroa, writing in 1615, lists Espinel among the leading performers and composers of the day and particularly associates his name with the guitar and with compositions known as *sonadas* and *cantares de sala*. The second of these terms may simply be a general one, "drawing-room songs" perhaps, referring to Espinel's popularity as a composer and performer for musical gatherings in the houses of notables, such as those meetings in Salamanca, Madrid, and Milan mentioned in *Marcos de Obregón*. On a number of occasions in the book, reference is made also to *sonadas* and we are given some idea of what this type of music, so closely associated with the name of Espinel, was like. For instance, as Marcos is on his way to Genoa, a prisoner on the ship of Marcello Doria, the musicians on board, accompanying themselves on guitars, sing verses based on the line: "The doubtful good, the sure and certain evil," a line taken from Espinel's "Sátira contra las damas de Sevilla" ("Satire on the Ladies of Seville") and the counter-tenor in the group indulges in improvised trills and flourishes woven around the melody line. In the final section of the novel, when the protagonist is describing musical evenings in the house of Antonio de Londoño in Milan and comparing them with those of Bernardo de Clavijo in Madrid, Marcos defends the view that song has lost none of its power to move its hearers to imitate the ideas contained within it. As an example he quotes an incident ⸰connected with one of his own *sonadas:* "Break the veins of the passionate breast," which is the first line of Liseo's lament in the "Egloga a don Hernando de Toledo" ("Eclogue to Don Hernando de Toledo"), one of the poems in Espinel's *Diversas rimas*. Such was the intensity of feeling expressed by the performer as he serenaded his beloved that she offered him a dagger to plunge into her breast in imitation of the song. Lope de Vega, in the *Laurel de Apolo (Laurels of Apollo)*, also pays tribute to effects achieved by Espinel in the performance of the same song. The anecdote may well be apocryphal but it does suggest that many of Espinel's poems were set to music and performed by him in the drawing-rooms — if not beneath the balconies — of the cultured society of the day.

In both cases, the songs are referred to as *sonadas* in the text, and Espinel describes the genre as having "a divine air and novelty." In an earlier episode, Marcos and a barber's boy also perform *sonadillas* in which the hero sings a bass harmony to the lad's melody line.

Again, there is the suggestion of improvised "throat passages" or trills interwoven around the tune. Isabel Pope Conant has suggested that the term *sonada* may have been used to describe the combination of a solo voice singing an independent melody line with chordal support on the five-stringed guitar, a musical genre foreshadowing the development of seventeenth-century monody. The association of Espinel's name with the five-stringed guitar could well have arisen because of his reputation in the salons of Madrid in connection with what really was an invention of his — the *sonada.*

It is also important to bear in mind that for twenty-five years Espinel was in charge of the music performed in the Capilla del Obispo of the Church of San Andrés in Madrid. He not only trained the choir and chose appropriate music for the services but also composed original music. He was skilled in plainsong, counterpoint, and the techniques of polyphony. Although, as in the case of the *sonadas,* no trace of the music remains, there is reference in a contemporary document to his working on three hymns and a mass in honor of St. Isidore, and the story goes that his anthems were still being performed in Ronda at the end of the seventeenth century.

It is clear from references to and by Espinel that he was considered one of the most versatile and talented musicians of the age. He was obviously familiar with the leading figures in musical circles in the capital, and his name was widely known as a performer, composer, and Church musician. Although no example of his music has survived, the various testimonies to his talent, the knowledge indicated by his disquisitions on music in *Marcos de Obregón,* and the obvious love of music which shines through his writing on the subject and even colors his imagery show that we would do well to bear his musical abilities in mind when trying to reach a balanced assessment of his place in the cultural spectrum of the Spain of his day and not allow his fame to rest on the alleged addition of a string to the guitar.

XIV *Reputation as a Poet*

We shall deal in the next chapter with Espinel's concrete achievements as a poet when we analyze critically the poems which make up his *Miscellaneous Verse.* What we are concerned with here is his reputation as a poet. In the area of his poetry, there is a curious similarity with his reputation as a musician. A supposed

invention, in this case the verse-form known as the *espinela*, has
tended to be the subject of critical controversy over the years and
thus has obscured other factors which offer a more solid basis for
assessment of his record as a poet.

The *espinela* is another term for the octosyllabic, ten-line stanza
familiarly known as the *décima*. The rhyme-scheme is: *abba:a
ccddc*, with a pause at the end of the fourth line. It is this pause
which constitutes the secret of the success of the *espinela* and makes
it particularly suitable, like the sonnet, for a lyrical statement involving a logical development of ideas from thesis to conclusion within a
short span of lines. Without the pause, we would be dealing with
two metrically independent five-line stanzas; with it, the pattern
changes to two four-line stanzas (*abba, cddc*) linked by two central
lines (*ac*) which anchor the two parts in sound and sense. The thesis
is outlined in the first four lines. There is then a change of pace as
the stanza moves into the development of the argument and the
proof. The lyrical possibilities of the *espinela* were quickly recognized, and the strophe was widely used by poets and dramatists
from the beginning of the seventeenth century, representing, as it
did, an answer in traditional meter to the challenge of the Italianate
forms which had earlier threatened to swamp the poetry of Spain. In
the drama, its use was extended from being "good for complaints,"
as Lope puts it in his *Arte nuevo de hacer comedias . . . (New Art of
Writing Plays . . .)*, to the point where, by 1623–24, Lope was using
it as much as the four-line *redondilla*. In the work of Tirso, Alarcón,
and Calderón, it was generally, in percentage terms, third in frequency, along with the five-line *quintilla*, after *redondillas* and the
ballad meter, the *romance*.[25]

As in the case of the addition of the fifth string to the guitar,
Espinel's cause was espoused by Lope who claimed for his "Master"
the honor of inventing the *espinela*. Without his support, it is doubtful whether so much attention would have been paid to the origins
of the form. In the Dedication to the *Caballero de Illescas (The
Gentleman of Illescas)*, in *La Circe*, in the *Laurel de Apolo (Laurels
of Apollo)*, in *La Dorotea*, Lope insists on Espinel's name being
associated with the strophe, as its inventor. Lope was not, however,
the first or the only contemporary to refer to Espinel's "invention"
of this verse form. Céspedes y Meneses, in his *Poema trágico del
Español Gerardo (Tragic Poem of the Spaniard Gerard)*, published
in 1615, seems to have been responsible for coining the term *es-*

pinela and gives one of the few examples of the form employed by the poet himself in the preliminaries to the work. Espinel's nephew, Jacinto de Espinel Adorno, in his pastoral novel *El premio de la constancia (The Reward of Constancy)*, which appeared in 1620, also praises the strophe and quotes "No hay bien que del mal me guarde" ("There is no good which can save me from evil"), which is the only *espinela* included in *Miscellaneous Verse*.

It is, however, stretching a point to say that Espinel "invented" the strophe. Sporadic occurrences of this type of *décima* have been registered pre-dating the earliest suggested date for the Espinel example (1574–75). There is, for instance, a poem by Juan de Mal Lara, the *Mística pasionaria (Mysticism of the Passion)*, in which an *espinela* is dedicated to each of the fourteen Stations of the Cross. This poem, if genuine, must have been written before 1571, the date of Juan de Mal Lara's death. Another early and less controversial example has been found in the work of Baltasar de Alcázar.

In order to place Espinel's contribution into perspective, it is perhaps better to see him as crystallizing and, with Lope's help, popularizing a form of the ten-line strophe which poets had been experimenting with and working toward from the days of the *Cancionero* poets.[26] Juan de Mena, the Marquis of Santillana, Juan del Encina, Gómez Manrique, Fernández de Heredia, and many others used various combinations of *quintillas, redondillas,* and *sextinas* in order to arrive at a satisfactory ten-line formula. It was left to Espinel to bring these experiments to fruition and lend his name to the result. It is worth remembering, however, that only a few examples by him have been left to us. It is perhaps only because of Lope's insistence that Espinel should have the credit for the invention that we associate the strophe with him. Cultivation of it by the major poets of the age ensured its place in the metrical canon of Castilian poetry.

And so we are left with a worthy but not outstanding poet, in an age of great poets, credited with the invention of a strophe that he does not seem to have much used, who enjoyed a prestige and influence seemingly out of proportion to his achievements. To help to explain this gap between reputation and performance we must have recourse to his other activities: his work as a book censor for the Inquisition, his membership of literary coteries, his musical activities, his reputation as a Latinist. As a poet, musician, and priest, he moved in the right circles, belonged to the best *academias;* he knew all the "best" people, and, in particular, his special relationship with Lope de Vega, the "monster of Nature" as he was called by Cervantes, earned him additional kudos and respect. As his *aprobaciones* indicate, he was well versed in Classical and Renaissance literary theory, especially Aristotle and Horace, and his cultivation of Latin verse obviously impressed contemporaries who refer to him, on many occasions, as an elegant poet in Latin and Spanish. Although it is doubtful whether Lope de Vega took formal lessons in Espinel's studio, there is no reason to question Lope's statement that he submitted his early poetic efforts in Latin to Espinel for comment and correction. It was widely known also that Espinel had translated Horace's *Ars Poetica (Art of Poetry).* He calls him "my master Horace" and was much influenced, as we can see in *Marcos de Obregón,* by his ideas on the aims of literature.

All these factors, then, combine to make Espinel an influential and respected figure, an arbiter of literary taste, a model of elegance in Latin and Spanish verse. His *aprobaciones* stress, time and time again, Classical concepts concerning the combination of teaching and entertainment in literature, the need for decorum, elegance, and simplicity of style, etc. These opinions represented, as it were, the official view of literature, and Espinel came to be respected as a spokesman for solid, traditional values. His contribution to the poetry of an age which numbered Fray Luis de León, Herrera, Lope de Vega, Quevedo, Góngora, and Calderón among its brightest stars does not bear a direct relationship to his reputation but is dependent, as we have seen, upon other factors.

XV *The Face in the Mirror*

At the age of about forty, Espinel described himself, in a verse epistle to a patron, the Marquis of Peñafiel,[27] as being monstrously stout, with a large face, a short, thick neck, a fat chest, short arms, a pot belly and as much waist as a stewpot. His hands were like crabs, his legs clumsy and stiff, making him walk like a duck, and his feet were swollen, with the skin rolling over his ankles. When a nun asked him for a portrait, he gave her a wine jug with a priest's hat on top. This cruelly unflattering yet humorous self-portrait is an example of that sharpness of tongue which gave us the "Satire on the Ladies of Seville" and which contributed to his troubles before his move to Madrid; it also illustrates the effects of the obesity and gout which affected him seemingly from his mid-thirties onward and which were eventually responsible for his death.

Coupled with this somewhat grotesque appearance, Espinel enjoyed a reputation for asperity which sprang, according to prevailing medical theory, from his choleric humor. In another verse epistle, included, like the first, in *Miscellaneous Verse*, but this time addressed to an ecclesiastical patron, the Bishop of Málaga,[28] he admits to a choleric way of talking and a tendency, in his youth, to speak his mind bluntly and bitingly to all and sundry. He was, he confesses, over-critical and slow to praise.

Both these poems belong to that difficult period of Espinel's life when, having returned to Ronda, he found himself in an uncongenial atmosphere, a victim of envy, cut off from his friends and a promising literary career in Madrid. The epistle to the Bishop of Málaga indicates an awareness of the problem of his temperament and a desire to put early failings behind him. At the same time, it shows the backbiting and envy which were to sour his return to his native city and make him a recalcitrant priest, unwilling to serve the parish to which he had been appointed. Reports on his conduct speak of his living well off his income and doing nothing to earn it. He is accused of leading a dissolute life, and of pride and insubordination. The letter sent by Dr. Padilla to the King in 1596 quotes an account which lists the crimes of the clerics of Ronda as perjury, dereliction of duty, sexual immorality, bribery, and backbiting. Presumably the anonymous informant was one of the envious worthies of Ronda of whom Espinel complains in his epistle to the Bishop.

There was enough truth in these stories for Espinel to be tried and fined by ecclesiastical authorities in 1598. The exact nature of his crimes is not specified, but one is entitled to assume that the informer's list indicates the area involved. Given Espinel's gout and his absenteeism, simony is more likely than concubinage. The punishment seems to have had a salutary effect. Espinel's fortunes changed, and he was considered sufficiently reformed for the Ronda episode not to stand in the way of his Madrid appointment. His exercise of his obligations in the Capilla del Obispo is in striking contrast to the absenteeism and negligence of his Ronda days. Fellow-clerics in Madrid thought highly enough of him to send him as their representative to negotiate with the tax authorities, and, in the fulfilment of his duties as examiner of books for the Inquisition, he became known as a "great censor." Lope, in the letter to the

Duke of Sessa, already mentioned, was able to say that he had put
his old asperity behind him. He seems, in his later years, to have
achieved that forbearance, that Spanish *paciencia*, which, according
to the epistle cited earlier, he admired so much in his protector,
Bishop Pacheco but was unable at that time to achieve.

There is a sense in which the years spent in Ronda from 1586 until
his departure for Madrid represent a watershed in Espinel's experience. Before that time, his restless spirit had taken him to many
places, and by his own admission, he had given free rein to his
pleasure-loving but abrasive temperament. The *Miscellaneous
Verse* offers us a poetic record of those years and of the frustration
and enmity of Ronda, its petty provincialism, its harsh climate, its
depressing effect upon the enthusiasm and sense of vocation of a
new priest.

Marcos de Obregón, by contrast, represents the memoirs of this
"turbulent priest," recollected in the tranquility of old age and of a
settled, fulfilling way of life. Espinel, wearing the mask of his creation, glosses the events of his life, using them to entertain his reader
and, at the same time, teach that lesson of *paciencia* which he
learned relatively late in life, largely through the bitter experience
of Ronda. It is a *paciencia* which the English "patience" does not
convey; it is for Espinel and his Catholic reading public a
philosophical and religious concept encompassing tolerance, com-
passion, and a disabused vision of human life in the context of eternity. The old narrator of *Marcos de Obregón* is different from the
poet of *Miscellaneous Verse.* He projects an image, formed in old
age, on to the events of his life, flattering his contemporaries and
presenting himself as an *honnête homme* (man of integrity). This is
one feature of *Marcos de Obregón* which distinguishes it from the
picaresque novel, with which genre it is often associated, and gives
it the flavor of an apologia. The face in Espinel's mirror at the end of
his life is the one he would like to have seen reflected in the earlier
phases of his life.

XVI   *Fact and Fiction*

The opening chronological table and the skeleton biography of
Espinel which follows it rely almost exclusively upon the documents
and external evidence collected by Haley. There are significant gaps
since little is known of the author's early years and of the period

between his studies in Salamanca and his visit to Italy in 1581. Apart from his university career, then, — and there is some doubt about the extent of that — the first thirty years of Espinel's life are largely undocumented. It is, of course possible to fill in this and other gaps by referring to Espinel's own work, since both *Miscellaneous Verse* and *Marcos de Obregón* "testify" to a love life, travels in Spain and Flanders, and to a period of captivity in Algiers. Normally this evidence would be acceptable in helping us to place an author against the background of events which shaped his life. In the case of Espinel, however, such a procedure brings special problems. *Marcos de Obregón* in particular and, to a lesser degree, *Miscellaneous Verse*, paint a picture of the author himself in which the colors of reality are heightened for literary effect. If we are to examine the procedures by which Espinel satirizes or romanticizes himself in *Miscellaneous Verse* and by which he rearranges the time-sequence of his life or uses a *Doppelgänger* effect in his portrayal of Marcos, it is important to establish the known facts of his career at the outset. In this way, poeticized or fictionalized autobiography can be set in a context of literary technique and not used to produce a fanciful version of Espinel's life as a starting-point for the study of his work.

CHAPTER 2

Diversas rimas

I The Poetic Scene

ESPINEL'S *Diversas rimas (Miscellaneous Verse)* was published
in 1591. The decade or so which preceded its appearance saw
the change-over between generations in the development of Golden
Age poetry.[1] By 1580, the Italianate tradition established by Boscán
and Garcilaso de la Vega had taken root in Spain, and Herrera, in his
commentary on Garcilaso's work, could review the achievements of
the new style over the past fifty years, set the standards for poets to
come, and confirm the status of Garcilaso as a classic. Also, by the
1580's we have seen the best or the last of such major figures as Luis
de León, San Juan de la Cruz, Luis de Camoens, and Francisco de
Aldana; Fernando de Herrera himself, although he lived until 1597,
published his *Algunas obras (Some Works)* in 1582 and is generally
taken to have written no new poems after that date. The same
decade heralds the birth of Quevedo and the first poems of Góngora, the two figures who dominate and shape the evolution of
Spanish poetry in the seventeenth century. Straddling the generation represented by Luis de León and Herrera and that of Góngora
and Quevedo are Espinel and Lope de Vega who, in the field of
poetry, looked upon the author of *Miscellaneous Verse* as his mentor. Although a minor figure as a poet in his own right, Espinel was a
much-respected arbiter of poetic taste and model of elegant versification. He stood at a major crossroads in Spanish poetry and his
Miscellaneous Verse is, among other things, a compendium of
themes and forms current in lyric poetry in the 1580's.

In order to place the work of any Golden Age poet in context, it is
important to recognize the continuity of the Peninsular poetic tradition from the Middle Ages until the beginning of the seventeenth
century. Firmly anchored to a body of accepted doctrine on love,

36

patriotism, religion, the structure of society, and the aims of literature, it purveys a basically medieval world-view from the fifteenth-
century *cancionero* poets through Garcilaso de la Vega and Luis de
León to the generation represented by Lope de Vega. For example,
the view of love inherited from the Provençal troubadours, with its
emphasis upon the superiority of the beloved, the courteous, humble servitude of the lover, and the cult of love to which he sub-
scribes, persists, with Neo-Platonic and Petrarchan overlays, into
the seventeenth century. *Cancionero* love poetry stresses the de-
licious agonies of the lover, the paradox of the death wish which
gives the poet a reason for being, the elegant ritual of the game of
love — all of which is reflected in the antitheses, word-play, and
stylization of the language. Obviously, subsequent centuries refine
the tradition, but the great love poetry of the Golden Age harks back
to this medieval view.

The courtly and popular streams of poetry, too, continue to run
side by side from the fifteenth century onward. The Marquis of
Santillana (1398–1458) may have considered the popular forms, such
as the ballad, as fit only to amuse the lower classes; only thirty years
or so after his death, Nebrija in his *Grámatica castellana (Castilian
Grammar)* had accepted the *romance* into the poetic canon and the
traditional meters continued to add vitality to the development of
poetry in Spain until the middle of the seventeenth century, co-
existing with the Italianate innovations. Indeed, one important aspect of this persistence of the traditional forms with which Espinel is
intimately connected is the stimulus given by the demand for musical settings of poems for court circles and gatherings in the houses of
rich patrons. The shorter, traditional line was widely used for these
pieces, which often took the form of a line-by-line gloss on an introductory stanza. Collections of these songs illustrate the important
contribution made by musicians like Espinel to the popularization of
traditional forms alongside the Italian meters. Religious *(a lo divino)*
glosses of popular poetry, which enjoyed a vogue during the
Counter Reformation, also show that the influx of Italian forms produced a healthy co-existence which is reflected in a typical collection such as *Miscellaneous Verse*.

The new and enriching element in this steady development,
then, is the introduction of meters and poetic ideas from Italy in the
second quarter of the sixteenth century. It was at the instigation of
Andrea Navagiero, the Venetian ambassador to Spain, that Juan

Boscán (1474?–1542) began to experiment with "sonnets and other
kinds of poetic forms used by the good authors of Italy." Spurred on
by his friend, Garcilaso de la Vega (1501?–36), Boscán abandoned
the traditional meters to devote himself to adapting the Italian hendecasyllable to Spanish poetry in new verse combinations such as
the *terza rima* (tercet), *ottava rima* (octave), *lira* (5-line stanza),
canzone (Petrarchan ode), and sonnet. A few sonnets by the Marquis of Santillana reflect an earlier Italian influence, but the efforts
of Boscán and Garcilaso de la Vega were decisive and, thanks to the
influence of Bembo, Petrarch became the model for the Italian *dolce
stil nuovo* which injected new blood into the body of Spanish poetry
in the early sixteenth century. Apart from the verse-forms already
mentioned, the Petrarchan tradition also brought with it a taste for
the pastoral eclogue, the epistle, and the elegy; a renewal of interest
in Virgil, Ovid, and Horace and in Classical myth, and an adaptation
of Neo-Platonic concepts to poetry.

After the formal contribution, however, perhaps the most important Italianate influence was in the realm of poetic theory. Poems
written within the Petrarchan tradition reflect the body of ideas on
the nature of the universe and the aims of literature which are the
legacy of Renaissance humanism. Neo-Platonism thus envisaged the
relationship of earth to heaven as that of a small world encompassed
by and linked to the macrocosm. The things of this world are seen as
reflections of divine archetypes. The Renaissance view of the aims of
poetry is colored by this conception of the nature of reality. Poetic
imagery, for example, has as its function to relate the particular to
the universal. The underlying aim of poetry and one which Espinel,
given his predilection for Horace, especially stressed (see Chapter
III, Section V), was that it should combine delight and instruction.
The union of the two is closer and more subtle than simply sugaring
a didactic pill; it involves reflecting in poetry the concept of the
harmony of the universe, outlined above, in the relationship between the purpose of a poem and the appropriateness of the terms
in which it is expressed. It is in this way that the Renaissance poet
seeks to express truth and imitate Nature, not in the sense of copy-
ing reality, as a photographer might do, but in order to relate, in an
ordered and artistically pleasing way, the particulars of the poetic
vision to the universal values which give it depth and meaning.
Imagery has a dual role to play in contributing to the pleasing artifice of a poem and in directing the reader's attention beyond im-

mediate enjoyment to the coherence and truth of the work in relation to the universal qualities which it reflects. The body of theory
upon which Renaissance poetry is based — of which the foregoing is
but an inadequate summary — stems, therefore, from an ordered,
hierarchical, and basically medieval view of the universe and, in
stressing precepts such as "dulce et utile" ("pleasant and useful"),
literary decorum, and the imitation of Nature, it gives rise to a type
of poetry whose artistry and seriousness of purpose can sometimes
be lost on a modern reader, unaware of the premises upon which it
is based. Even the work of a minor poet like Espinel can acquire
greater depth and meaning if these assumptions are borne in mind.

II *The Composition of the Collection*

As a number of the poems in the collection show, the preparation
of *Miscellaneous Verse* coincided with the poet's return to his home
town of Ronda in 1586 (see Chapter 1, Sections VI–VII) to begin a
checkered career as a provincial priest in which his absences in
Madrid over the succeeding thirteen years landed him in trouble
with the ecclesiastical authorities.[2] Espinel obviously prepared the
first draft of the collection during 1586, since the volume has an
aprobación signed by Alonso de Ercilla of January 7, 1587. It originally consisted of pieces already written, such as the elegiac sonnets
in memory of Ana de Austria, and poems especially composed, as in
the case of the "Canción a su patria" ("Song to His Homeland"), to
celebrate his return to Ronda or to lament the recent death of his
mother, as with the "Elegía a la muerte de su madre" ("Elegy on the
Death of His Mother"). Inexplicably, however, the license granted
to Espinel to publish his work at that time was not used and it was
not until 1591 that *Miscellaneous Verse* appeared in print. Internal
evidence shows that the four-year delay was a bitter period in Espinel's life, and he added some poems to the miscellany, possibly
suppressing others to make room, which reflect the disillusion he
felt. His verse epistles to Dr. Luis de Castilla and to the Marquis of
Peñafiel indicate his difficulties in finding a patron and in adapting
himself to the small-town atmosphere of Ronda. His attitude
changed from that of returning prodigal, glad to be back in his home
town, to that of the reluctant priest whose artistic ambitions were
being stifled by the pettifogging attitudes and jealousy of his fellow-
clerics.

Miscellaneous Verse was prepared, then, during an unhappy but decisive period in the personal life of Espinel; it also came (see Section I of this chapter) at an important stage in the development of Golden Age poetry. In both respects, the collection has a retrospective air: it offers a poetic review of Espinel's early years, concentrating upon a narrow band in the 1580's (his travels and sojourn in Italy, his return to Ronda, and entry into the priesthood); these poems also provide a survey of what Spanish poetry was like in the 1580's in terms of themes and structures, before the full impact of Góngora and Quevedo was felt. It may, perhaps, be worth pointing out that studies of literature tend to concentrate too much upon masterpieces. Here we have a typical collection of the poems of the first half of the career of a minor poet who, in later life was highly regarded as an accomplished and elegant versifier, acknowledged by Lope de Vega as his poetic mentor and deferred to as a "great censor" of books for the Inquisition. We see him filtering the expeiiences of youth and of a tumultuous period in his life through the fine mesh of his poetic vision and producing a series of poems which bring into play most of the traditional and Italianate meters and stanzas available to a poet of the day. There is a sense in which *Miscellaneous Verse* may be regarded as a poetic manual of the 1580's.

III   *Preliminaries to the Volume*

Espinel's verse miscellany was published under the patronage of the Duke of Alba to whom the poet addressed an elegy on the death of his illustrious predecessor (195–99) and some dedicatory tercets (33–34). Setting aside the usual mock-humility of an author vis-à-vis his patron, we see Espinel displaying his wares before the Duke and urging him, as he does the reader of the *Marcos de Obregón,* to look beneath the surface of the simple verses and pastoral format for the poet's intentions in writing the work. "Amid crags and rugged mountains," Espinel writes cryptically of another time when he went blindly and heedlessly through life and his "bold Muse" prepares to sing its sad song. Perhaps, then, we can expect *Miscellaneous Verse* to shed some light on those ill-documented early years when Espinel's conduct seems to have been a source of regret to him in later life. At all events, the poet hints that the eclogues and other poems have more than a conventional and surface interest to while away the hours of the Duke's exile.

For the rest, the preliminaries of *Miscellaneous Verse* are conventional enough. Alonso de Ercilla, in approving the volume, says that the lyrical poetry is among the best he has seen and Alonso de Valdés, secretary to a gentleman-in-waiting to the King, contributes an essay on poetry designed to impress with its erudition and stimulate patronage for the arts. This is followed by the usual collection of laudatory poems by friends of the author, full of puns on Espinel's name and comparing him to Pindar and Tasso. It is interesting to note, among this list of panegyrists, the names of Lupercio Leonardo de Argensola and Lope de Vega who were almost certainly members with Espinel of the same literary academies, such as the Academia de Madrid sponsored by another of the contributors, Don Félix Arias Girón; also included is the latter's lover, Doña Catalina Zamudio, daughter of Agustina de Torres, whose musical soirées in Salamanca Espinel remembers in *Marcos de Obregón*. This circle of literary and musical friends will be widened when we come to consider the longest poem in the collection, "La casa de la Memoria" ("The House of Memory").

IV   *Versification*

Miscellaneous Verse offers the reader a register of the meters and verse-forms available to a poet of the second half of the sixteenth century in Spain, embracing a whole range of possibilities for the Italian hendecasyllabic line used on its own or in combination with the heptasyllable, together with the traditional Castilian meters in which the eight-syllable line dominates.[3] In order to illustrate the variety of combinations achieved, capitals have been used below to represent hendecasyllables, and small letters for the shorter, traditional lines.

Espinel includes thirty-six sonnets in his collection. Only three show any departure from the standard rhyme-scheme of: *ABBA ABBA CDE CDE*, based on the Petrarchan model and favored by Garcilaso, Herrera, Cervantes, Góngora, and Lope de Vega in his early works. Two of the variants have tercets which run: *CDC DCD* (45, 46), as in the interlinked rhymes of the *terza rima*, and represent the preferred pattern of the later Lope, together with

Quevedo, Villamediana and Calderón. The final variation: *CDE CED* (177), in which the rhymes in the final tercet are transposed, is not listed by Navarro Tomás among the most common schemes in use among the poets of the Golden Age. For his translation of Horace's "Quis multa gracilis" (175), Espinel uses the standard rhyme-scheme but with a tailpiece or *estrambote* of three lines (*efF*). A further legacy from Italian poetry, as well as the sonnet, is the *terza rima* (tercet), chiefly used in longer poems such as the verse epistle and the elegy. Famous examples from the period are Fernández de Andrada's "Epístola moral a Fabio" ("Moral Epistle to Fabio"), Quevedo's epistle to the Conde-Duque de Olivares and Herrera's elegy "No bañes en el mar sagrado y cano" ("Do not immerse in the white and holy sea"). The tercet was also used in the plays of the period for serious monologues. The form consists of hendecasyllables linked by rhyme in groups of three: *ABA BCB CDC*, etc., and Espinel employs it, in common with other poets of his day, for the two elegies and five epistles included in the miscellany. He also uses the hendecasyllable, this time in eight-line stanzas rhyming *ABABABCC* (octavas reales), for two love poems (51–52, 117–18) and for the most ambitious work in the collection, "La casa de la Memoria" ("The House of Memory"; 78–95). Cervantes similarly wrote his panegyrical "Canto de Calíope" ("Song of Calíope") in octave form; this adaptation of the Italian *ottava rima* was used in the Golden Age theater to lend weight and dignity to recitals of past events or to ceremonial scenes and also became the standard vehicle for the literary epic and the long narrative poem. The Spanish word for "stanza" (*estancia*) is given to the combination of eleven- and seven-syllable lines to form the equivalent of the Petrarchan ode or *canzone*. The stanzas can vary in length from the five-line *lira (aBabB)* to the twenty-line verses of Garcilaso de la Vega's fourth *Canción*. Espinel's anthology contains ten such *canciones*, ranging from the six-line strophes of his song of absence, "En soledad y ausencia" ("In solitude and absence"; 135–37), which are arranged as follows: *aBaBcC*, to the fifteen-line stanzas of his "Canción a su patria" ("Song to His Homeland"; 68–73) which run: *ABCABCcDDefFEgG*. The *canción* is also a favored form for use in the pastoral eclogue, which was brought into vogue in Spain by Garcilaso. Espinel includes four eclogues in *Miscellaneous Verse*. In one of them, the "Egloga Liseo" (63–66), he uses a *canción* stanza of fifteen lines: *ABcCABddEEFfGFG*; in the other three, he employs a combination of Italianate meters including tercets, octaves, *canción* stanzas of from eleven to sixteen lines and hendecasyllabic blank verse known in Spanish prosody as *silva*. The six-line *canción* stanza *(aBaBcC)*, which was based on the *lira* and used by Luis de León, was adopted by Espinel for his translation of the Horace ode included in the collection (124–25).

Although, as can be seen from the foregoing, Espinel displays an impressive technical command of the Italian meters based upon the Italian hendecasyllable, some of his best effects are achieved in the poems which feature short-line, traditional meters. His "Endechas" ("Dirge") (187–89) lamenting the loss of a lady's favor, for example, consist of twenty-one quatrains of six-syllable lines rhyming: *abba*. This form is referred to by Navarro Tomás as "minor *redondillas*" because of the resemblance to the octosyllabic quatrain which is the cornerstone of the Castilian metrical system.[4] The minor *redondillas* were cultivated by Hurtado de Mendoza and Francisco de la Torre for amatory laments, and in Espinel's hands, the *endechas* have an unforced simplicity and flow which places them among the poet's best work.

The term "redondilla" was used in the Golden Age to describe not only a quatrain of eight-syllable lines, rhyming either *abba* or *abab*, but also, in the second half of the sixteenth century, longer stanzas of octosyllables which were known as "*redondillas* of five (six, seven etc.) lines." Espinel, in the section dedicated to Castilian forms, gives us several examples, from the standard *abba* quatrains of the jocular "Redondillas a una lima" (Quatrains to a Lime"; 183–84) and the five-line *quintillas* of "A unas lágrimas" ("To Some Tears"; 184–85) to the only example in *Diversas rimas (Miscellaneous Verse)*, *pace* Navarro Tomás,[5] of the ten-line *décima* which came to bear Espinel's name, the *espinela*: "No hay bien que del mal me guarde" ("There is no good which can save me from evil"; 172–74). Since we have already given a detailed analysis of the *espinela* in the previous chapter (see Section XIV), there is no need to dwell further on it here. Instead, it might be worth highlighting another ten-line combination with an innovatory ring. This is used for Espinel's "Volved pensamiento mío" ("Recover, thoughts of mine"; 169–71), which is made up of *redondillas de diez versos* in which the third and sixth lines are short *pies quebrados* or irregular measures. The rhyme-scheme is thus: *abaabccddc*. This shorter line produces an attractive, syncopated effect in the flow of the stanza, allowing a pause for

thought or emphasis every few lines. Espinel is outstanding, however, in the use of eight-, nine- and ten-line strophes of octosyllables
to gloss an initial group of lines *(estribillo)*, repeating each of its lines
in turn as part of the commentary or elaboration. He uses the term
redondillas for the initial stanza and *coplas* ("verses") for the gloss;
he does not use the word *villancico* ("carol") by which such songs
were commonly known. There are seventeen examples of this type
of composition, ranging from the simple humor of "Mil veces voy a
hablar" ("A thousand times do I approach"; 194–95) to the ingenious
paradoxes of "Son mis tormentos crecidos" ("My torments are in-
creased"; 177–78) and the legal images of "Tiempo turbado y perdido" ("Time of upset and loss"; 180–81). It is tempting to assume
that, although Espinel's music has been lost, here at least are *coplas*
which were intended to be sung, just as were the lost octaves which
glossed "El bien dudoso, el mal seguro y cierto" ("The doubtful
good, the sure and certain evil") from Espinel's "Sátira contra las
damas de Sevilla" ("Satire on the Ladies of Seville")[6] and Liseo's
lament, "Rompe las venas del ardiente pecho" ("Break the veins of
the passionate breast"; 106–09), which forms part of the "Egloga a
don Hernando de Toledo el Tío" ("Eclogue to Don Hernando of
Toledo, the Uncle"). Certainly these accomplished glosses would
lend themselves to a musical setting and represent some of the best
poetry in the collection.

Editions and anthologies of Golden Age poetry usually relegate
the details of versification to the status of an appendix to the introduction. In the case of *Miscellaneous Verse*, however, we have given
some prominence to the technical aspect of Espinel's poetry in
order to give the reader an impression of the scope of the collection
and because one of the important aspects of the work is precisely the
range of its coverage of the traditional and Italianate lines and
strophes available to a poet in the 1580's. In his later years, Espinel's use of certain verse-forms was considered an object lesson for
younger poets, and it is interesting to see him experimenting with
and perfecting a variety of meters and strophes, probing the possibilities of each: the way to develop an argument, stage by stage,
through the quatrains and first tercet of a sonnet to reach a pithy
conclusion in the last lines; the achievement of a flowing rhythm by
clever use of the chained rhymes of the *terza rima;* the majesty of
the *octavas* in the description of "caverns measureless to Man" in
the first canto of "La casa de la Memoria;" the effects secured by the

combination of line-lengths in the *canciones* and of different types of strophe in the eclogues; the unforced simplicity of the *endechas* and the agility and grace of the glosses — all these qualities might well have served to enhance Espinel's reputation as a poet in the literary academies and influential circles of the Madrid to which, at the time of the publication of *Miscellanous Verse*, he longed to escape.

V A Poetic Confession

In the opening and closing sonnets of the collection, Espinel indicates to his reader that the poems are a verse record of his youthful folly and an acknowledgement that he has learned his lesson: in "Estas son las reliquias, fuego y yelo" ("These are the last vestiges, fire and ice"; 45), he vaguely refers to a headlong flight along a discreditable path, only to draw back just in time; the final sonnet, "Del cauteloso y miserable engaño" ("Of the cunning and wretched deception"; 200–201), ends with the hope that the poet's work will serve as an example: "That all is vanity, all is folly" (201). In both poems, Espinel uses the word *desengaño* ("disillusion") to describe his awakening to the error of his ways. If one assumes that the arrangement of the poems in the miscellany is not haphazard, then the prominence given to these sonnets underlines the confessional aspect. At the same time, however, it is as well to point out the nonspecific nature of the poet's sins—there are no dates, places, or names, just vague references to being in "dire straits" (45) or to "flattering treatment" and "singular harshness" (200). This lack of precision is a clue to the value and danger of seeing *Miscellaneous Verse* as what Haley calls a "poetic diary" of Espinel's early life and, in particular, of the 1580's. On the one hand, it is possible, through the poems, to chart the poet's youthful wildness: his sojourn in Italy, as attested by the *canción* (149–51) and the three sonnets (151–52) in memory of Ana de Austria; his return to Spain and entry into the priesthood (perhaps the "choice of a new station" [175] referred to in one of the glosses?); the change of attitude toward Ronda reflected in the joyous "Canción a su Patria" ("Song to His Homeland"; 68–73); and the bitterness of the epistles to the Bishop of Málaga (73–77) and the Marquis of Peñafiel (155–62). On the other hand, we can weave a romantic story out of some of the imprecise allusions of *Miscellaneous Verse*, supplemented by episodes from *Marcos de Obregón* and a lot of imagination, which will show the young Espinel spending a wild year in Seville drinking, womanizing, being pursued by the law, or paying court to Doña Antonia Maldonado y Calatayud, only for her to reject him in favor of a more acceptable suitor. In spite of the well-documented biography by Haley, there are still gaps in our knowledge of Espinel's doings at certain periods. There are obvious dangers in programing Espinel to fit fictional or poetic exploits designed to fill those gaps. Where the collection does ring true, however, is as a register of feelings, which according to Rousseau is the truest form of autobiography: the contrition regarding a misspent youth, the agony and ecstasy of love, the nostalgia and heartbreak of absence, the joy of homecoming, the bitterness of spoilt hopes, the rueful admission of a wayward temperament. All these moods are in the collected poems and give certain sections of the work a confessional tone. It emerges in these moments of examination of conscience, not so much as a poetic diary of Espinel's early years, as a generalized confession of feelings regarding the past. Whereas *Marcos de Obregón* fictionalizes Espinel's past, his poetry confesses the sins of the years up to his entry into the priesthood.

The confession is, first of all, one of personal failure, as indicated in the opening sequence of sonnets. In the sonnet, "En el Abril de mis floridos años" ("In the April of my golden years"; 45), Espinel sees himself as an Icarus figure, fired by early literary ambitions only to find his pen not equal to the task. His major weakness of character is a tendency to go to extremes: "Osando temo, estoy helado y ardo" ("Daring, I am full of fear, I am frozen and yet burn"; 45), as the third sonnet in the collection puts it. These extremes, although they coincide with a Petrarchan love cliché, in Espinel's case are corroborated by medical evidence and by the record of his asperity in dealing with his fellow-clerics.[7] The fourth sonnet, "Duerme el desnudo en la desierta playa" ("The naked man sleeps on the deserted shore"; 46), paints a picture of an Espinel, Sisyphus-like, unable to rest because of his conscience, a prey to: "Snakes, tigers and the furies of Hell" (46).

The initial series of sonnets, then, sets the scene for the confessional aspect. The verse-epistle to the Bishop of Málaga (73–77) is the nearest Espinel comes to a full-scale poetic confession. It was written about 1586, around the time when the poet, thanks to the support of the Bishop, became a full-fledged priest and, as well as the expected flattery of a patron, the letter has a human appeal as

Espinel sadly enumerates his physical and moral defects: his hoarse voice, staccato manner of talking, hasty character, youthful indiscretions, asperity in judgment. There is, however, a sense in which Espinel feels "more sinned against than sinning." After all, ". . . I am not an angel, but a man" (74); and although he feels "burning regret" (74) for the sins of his youth, in Ronda they will not forgive and forget. He has become the victim of the blind, cancerous envy of fat-bellied pork-butchers and verminous nobodies (75–76) who cannot leave him alone. The vituperative sting of the paraphrase is a measure of Espinel's indignation. The reader can feel the poet's gorge rise as he gives way, once again, to the choleric temperament which has haunted him all his life. Then, however, mindful of his task, Espinel controls himself and appeals to his patron for guidance. He realizes that he must learn that "patience" (77) and courage which Bishop Pacheco abundantly possesses. In other words, the lesson is the same in 1586, when Espinel was putting together his *Miscellaneous Verse*, as it was in 1614–16, when he was composing *Marcos de Obregón: paciencia*, because this life is but a "breve sogno" ("short dream"; 77) in the context of eternity.

The change of attitude toward Ronda is a notable feature of *Miscellaneous Verse:* The "Canción a su Patria" ("Song to His Homeland"; 68–73), for example, is an emotional tribute to historic Ronda, set amid its mountains, from a native son returning to dedicate the autumn of his days to pastoral duties under Bishop Pacheco. "Health, peace and happiness" (73) are what Espinel seeks. He fails on all three counts, and the allusions to "envy" (70) and the "blessed clergy" (73) have an ironic flavor in the light of later events (see Chapter 1, Section VI). The "Elegía a la muerte de su madre" ("Elegy on the Death of His Mother"; 146–49) also paints an emotional picture of a Ronda deprived of the saintliness of the poet's mother and makes no mention of the unpleasantness to come in the freshness and Dantesque horror of its grief. Two later epistles, however, written as Espinel was putting the finishing touches to his volume and casting round for a patron for the work, take up the story where the letter to Bishop Pacheco left off. "Al Doctor Luis de Castilla" (119–23) is a somewhat blatant appeal for patronage addressed to the Duke of Alba's steward. Since *Miscellaneous Verse* eventually appeared under the aegis of the Duke, one may suppose that the epistle played its part. Espinel, faced with the loss of his Maecenas, Bishop Pacheco, who had been appointed to Cordova, was obviously nervous that he would be left unprotected against the evil tongues and ingratitude of Ronda which: "Never valued me as a dear possession" (122). Other places, the poet bitterly observes, think of him as a Midas or an Apollo, but in Ronda he is poor and ill-regarded. Giving an account of himself in the "Carta a Don Juan Téllez Girón, Marqués de Peñafiel" ("Letter to Don Juan Téllez Girón, Marquis of Peñafiel"; 155–62), Espinel again becomes vituperative on the subject of his home town. In Ronda, he tells the Marquis, the talk is mostly of "Pigs and acorns, sheep and scab" (156); the rest is poisonous gossip. Espinel is furious at the way he has been treated: "The one who should be my mother, is my stepmother,/ The one who bore me is my chief executioner" (157). And yet, Espinel manages to conquer his indignation and, having brought the Marquis up to date by describing the recent explosion and fire at the powder factory in Granada, embarks on a satirical self-portrait (see Chapter 1, Section XV) which says much for his ability to laugh at himself.

This, then, is the Espinel who emerges from the confessional verse: a man of violent temperament, racked by conscience over the excesses of his youth, frustrated in his ambitions, and bitterly disappointed at the cold reception he had on his return to Ronda. He is shown to be aware of his faults and desperately seeking to acquire that *paciencia* which is crucial also to an understanding of the message of *Marcos de Obregón*, desperately trying, also, to escape from the pettiness and envy of Ronda to the capital where he feels his talents will be appreciated. As a poetic assessment of Espinel as he approaches forty, it is, in terms of mood and feelings rather than places and dates, a good likeness.

VI   *Célida and Liseo*

In Golden Age love poetry, it was common practice for the poet to adopt literary pseudonyms for his beloved as a cloak for his Petrarchan outpourings.[8] The elaborate game of love, with the luckless lover grieving over the hardness of heart of his lady, was played out, as in a *bal masqué*, behind a symbolic disguise which gave an air of mystery and elegance to the ritualized movements. Thus, in the literary academies and soirées, poems would be read and circulated in which Lope de Vega became Belardo, Mira de Amescua was Lisardo, Pedro Liñán de Riaza, Riselo, and Pedro Laynez, Tirsi (see

"Canción a Pedro Laynez"; 128–32); Quevedo addressed a series of love sonnets to Lisi, and among the many poets who laid claim to the name Filis for the subject of their adoring verses were Lupercio Leonardo de Argensola, Francisco de la Torre and Francisco de Rioja, while Belisa, Amarilis and Filida reflected the range of Lope's interests. Espinel who, as "La casa de la Memoria" ("The House of Memory") testifies, moved in the same circles as most of the above writers, adopted the name Liseo and chose Célida and Ninfa as the poetic names of the object of his "secret passion" (63).

In the opening sequence of sonnets in *Miscellaneous Verse*, Espinel gradually reveals to the reader the strength of his attachment to Ninfa-Célida, having first, as we saw in the previous section, issued warnings about youthful folly, the dashing of hopes, and the pangs of conscience. She gradually takes shape through a series of sonnets which describe the attributes of a beautiful woman without naming her: the "white ivory" (46) of her hands, the "angelic voice" (47), the hair like "divine strands of gold" (47) rivaling the sun. The idealization is such that it could be anybody. Then, in the ninth sonnet, this goddess of beauty acquires a name: Ninfa. We see her in "Cogiendo va, y llevando al blanco seno" ("She is gathering and taking to her white bosom"; 48) picking herbs, with Nature blossoming where she trod in anger. The colors of Nature, a feature of Espinel's verse which links him to Herrera, are associated with the appearance of the beloved before the waiting Liseo, like "The glory of the world" (48) in the sonnet which follows, "El bermellón a manchas se mostraba" ("Vermilion in patches was appearing"; 48–49); but the ecstasy of that moment is tempered by the thought, contained in "Estrechos lazos, que el mortal e indigno [Cuerpo]" ("Tight bonds which the mortal and unworthy [Body]"; 49), that the most propitious occasion for love can be turned into a disaster by Ninfa's harshness. It is not until the thirteenth sonnet in the collection, however, "Si el Teucro París da la poma de oro" ("If the Trojan Paris gives the golden apple"; 49), that Liseo's beloved appears as Célida, amid the gods and goddesses of mythology, to be thrice rewarded for her "prudence, grace and beauty" (49).

It is at this stage, having used the opening sonnets to hint that the youthful adoration of Célida was an aberration and to keep the reader in suspense concerning the true nature of his passion, that Espinel, in a series of more ambitious poems, begins to elaborate on the Liseo-Célida affair. In a pastoral setting, the poet in the *canción*

"Tierno pimpollo, nueva y fértil planta" ("Tender sapling, new and fertile plant"; 49–51) sings the praises of the beloved, reminding her, again with many allusions to Classical myth, that her severity causes her lover suffering. A similar situation is presented in the octaves which follow, "Nuevos efectos de milagro extraño" ("New effects of awesome wonder"; 51–52). Ninfa's *rigor*, coupled with her worth and beauty, "Freezes the fire when it burns hottest in me" (51). This is the dilemma and the paradox of the Petrarchan lover. As the *canción* "Si en esa clara luz pura y serena" ("If in that clear light, pure and serene"; 57–60) makes clear, the lover fell innocently into Célida's trap, and now, because of her beauty and her coldness, chance meetings bring him joy and despair: "I came to know your harshness and my good fortune" (60). The only weapon the enslaved poet has is to remind his beloved, as he does in the epistle "El aspereza, que el rigor del cielo" ("The harshness which the severity of heaven"; 60–63) that even perfect beauty such as hers does not last forever.

The Liseo-Célida affair reaches its greatest heights — and depths — in Espinel's pastoral eclogues. The "Liseo Eclogue" (63–66) portrays the shepherd weeping inconsolably amid the beauties of Nature as he apostrophizes his beloved Célida from whom he is separated. Repeated questions emphasize his anguish as he remembers her loveliness. His misery finally overcomes him; he swoons and is carried off by his companions to a place "Amid jasmine, roses and amaranth" (66) where he can recover sufficiently to continue his lament. Liseo's cry from the heart in the "Egloga a don Hernando de Toledo el Tío" ("Eclogue to Don Hernando of Toledo, the Uncle"; 104–16) is that same "Rompe las venas del ardiente pecho" ("Break the veins of the passionate heart") which is quoted in *Marcos de Obregón* as an example of how song can so impress that the listener may be moved to imitate the situation being described. Such is Liseo's obsession that "Célida is everything, he meditates upon Célida" (106), and his case reminds us of the love-religion of Calisto in the *Celestina*, although in his account of the relationship with Célida, Liseo makes it clear that his love was "without any element of foul and immoral intent" (111) and achieved a oneness in Nature that Calisto and Melibea's tragic liaison lacked: "When the dogs of her flock saw me,/ They would come out, wagging their tails, to greet me./ My lambs, if they saw her,/ Would lick Célida's feet and hands" (112). The idyll, however, is ruined by a "friend" who spread slander about the two and the fury of Célida hit Liseo like a lonely traveler caught in a storm. The later eclogue "Ay, apacible y sosegada vida" ("Oh peaceful and quiet life"; 137–46) offers a Horatian eulogy of the simple life, away from the cares of "royal palaces" (138), and Liseo, "all passion spent," is able to offer advice to his fellow-shepherds whose obsession with the beloved does not respond to the voice of reason or experience. The poet seems to be taking up the warning of the opening sonnets of *Miscellaneous Verse* against the dangers of spoiling the promise of youth and indicating, in the final stanzas of the eclogue, that it is possible to worship beauty from afar and amid the peace of Nature; he seems to be advocating a philosophical detachment from the things of this world which eschews the excesses of swooning at the sight of the beloved and is wary of the faithlessness of women. It is a message which fits well with the burden of *Marcos de Obregón*'s emphasis on patience and fortitude.

The pattern of sentiments thus described, from the initial enslavement of the lover through his eyes and ears as he sees and listens to his beloved, through the agonies of disdain, to the final rejection and search for peace, has a long literary ancestry. Ovid, Virgil, and Horace have all made their contribution, along with figures from the Petrarchan tradition, the *Cancionero* poets, Ausías March, León Hebreo, Garcilaso, etc. By following in such distinguished footsteps, Espinel is joining in the Renaissance exploration of the paradox of love and the impossible search for perfection. The universality of application of his poetic findings is diminished by efforts to give a real-life identity to Célida. On the basis of a single reference in *Marcos de Obregón*, in which the beauty and gentleness of the wife of the Squire's host, on one of his adventures, are said to be "the living image of Doña Antonia Calatayud" (II, 178), Pérez de Guzmán constructed a platonic love affair between Doña Antonia Maldonado y Calatayud and Espinel. Their relationship, elaborated upon by Dorothy Clotelle Clarke, is supposed to have ended when the lady rejected Espinel in favor of a more acceptable suitor, Don Rodrigo de Céspedes, whom she later married. It was this unhappy love affair, so the legend goes, which caused the author to kick over the traces in Seville and eventually go to Italy. Viewed in this light, the Liseo-Célida poems become, along with *Marcos de Obregón*, a hunting-ground for biographical data which serve to put flesh on the bones of the unsubstantiated relationship. Literary detective work of this kind detracts from the casuistical exploration of the paradoxes of love and the hymn to beauty which are the major preoccupations of the poet in the Célida poems of *Miscellaneous Verse*. In the absence of hard evidence, it seems more likely that Liseo and Célida cover not a real but an idealized relationship, a poet's dream. We would, perhaps, do well to remember the words of Don Quixote, already quoted (see Chapter 1, Section VII), concerning the Phyllises and Amaryllises scattered through the pages of the imaginative literature of the Golden Age. As Quevedo puts it in the last line of one of his love sonnets: "I am an eternal lover of an eternal beloved."

VII   *The Espinel Circle*

A study of *Miscellaneous Verse* more rewarding than the search for traces of Doña Antonia Maldonado y Calatayud is one where corroboration is sought for Espinel's literary friendships and for his search for patronage among men of title and influence at the early stage of his career represented by the collection. The names gleaned from an examination of the poems and dedications also give an indication of his travels, of his yearning to leave Ronda, and his natural affinities with the social, literary, and musical life of Madrid.

The "Egloga a Ottavio Gonzaga" (Eclogue to Ottavio Gonzaga"; 96–104), for example, and the *canción*, "A Doña Sicilia de Medicis" ("To Lady Cecilia de Medici"; 133–35), reflect Espinel's stay in Italy where, until Gonzaga's death in 1583, he enjoyed the protection of the general. He showed his appreciation by an elaborate eclogue in which the virtues of the soldier's life are extolled over those of the shepherd's and by the song in praise of the beauty of Gonzaga's future wife. According to the evidence of *Marcos de Obregón* (I,45; II,196), Espinel sailed from Genoa to Barcelona in the company of Don Fernando de Toledo and his dedication of a major eclogue (104–16) to him is a measure, confirmed elsewhere, of the author's desire to ingratiate himself with the Albas. *Miscellaneous Verse* itself, as we have seen (see Section III of this chapter), is dedicated to the Duke of Alba and contains an elegy on the death of the former Duke (195–99); one of the poet's less tactful pleas for patronage is addressed to the Duke's steward, Dr. Luis de Castilla

(119–23), after Espinel learns in 1587 that his "sacred Maecenas" (119), Bishop Pacheco, is going to Cordova. Notwithstanding his fulsome praise in the epistle addressed to his ecclesiastical protector, the Bishop of Málaga (73–77) and the moving tribute in the *canción* "A Fray Rodrigo de Arce" ("To Brother Rodrigo de Arce"; 152–55) to the work of the Mercedarian friend of his youth in ransoming captives from the infidel, Espinel's interests are in the capital and it is toward engineering his escape from Ronda that some of his dedications are directed. The "Letter to Don Juan Téllez Girón, Marquis of Peñafiel" (155–62), for example, complains of the rusticity and harsh climate of Ronda and, as in other poems aimed at interesting aristocratic patrons in his case, gives an illustration of his descriptive powers by a vivid account of the explosion at a powder factory in Granada in 1590.

The second canto of "La casa de la Memoria" ("The House of Memory") shows how generous Espinel can be in his tributes to the distinguished men of arms and letters of his day and to the musicians, male and female, whose work he admired. By collating the list of writers in "The House of Memory" with the names of contributors of dedicatory poems to the volume as a whole and with those of the writers who collaborated in the preliminaries of such collections as López Maldonado's *Cancionero*, we can deduce the composition of a group of writers with whom Espinel seems to have had especially close relations.[9] Apart from López Maldonado himself, they are: Cervantes, Lope de Vega, the Argensola brothers, Pedro de Montesdoca, Liñán de Riaza, Pedro de Padilla and Pedro Laynez, to whom a *canción* (128–32) is also dedicated in *Miscellaneous Verse*. These, it would seem, are the figures whose company Espinel sought in the literary coteries of Madrid; it is with these writers that one finds Espinel's name associated in dedications, *aprobaciones*, and panegyrical references. Of this group, special mention has already been made (see Chapter 1, Section X) of Lope de Vega. Twelve years the junior of Espinel, Lope de Vega looked upon the older poet as his mentor and, in later years, repaid his debt handsomely by his warm tributes to Espinel's poetic abilities in Latin and Spanish; it was largely thanks to the propaganda efforts of Lope that the *décima* came to be known as the *espinela* and that Espinel enjoyed a reputation as a model of elegance and good taste in poetry.

VIII   *The Other Voice*

The arrangement of the poems is not so haphazard as might at first appear. Leaving aside the occasional "Elegía en la muerte del Duque de Alba" ("Elegy on the Death of the Duke of Alba"; 195–99) and the closing sequence of sonnets, both of which have counterbalancing verse at the beginning of the volume, Espinel dedicates a whole section late in the collection to poems in traditional meters. In these verses, based upon the shorter, mainly eight-syllable line, Espinel sets aside the mask of the anguished Petrarchan lover and the mantle of the seeker after patronage and in a more direct and straightforward poetic language talks of life and love. We are no longer in the cultured world of the Garcilasan eclogue, the love sonnet, or the Petrarchan ode but in a world where poems, the best of which resemble those of Lope de Vega, capture the cadences of popular speech and were probably meant to be sung. It is not the world of Célida (who scarcely rates the "tribute of a passing sigh") and Liseo, but of the more down-to-earth Alcida and Bras. Typical of the poet's attitude toward love in this section is the gloss on "Ya no me congojan tanto" ("Now they do not cause me so much anguish"; 192–93). The *estribillo* or refrain might be translated as follows: "Now they do not cause me so much anguish/ On my honor, Bras, these love affairs,/ Now I am recovering my spirit,/ Now I rejoice and play and sing" (192). In the final stanza of the gloss, Espinel expands on this thought: "There is no sadness or grief in me,/ Nor reasons for chagrin,/ Jealousy, passion or affliction./ Now all is happiness and pleasure,/ Now I rejoice and play and sing" (193). This does not mean, of course, that these traditional songs are uniformly gay; it does mean that the antitheses and conceits are less tortured and there is more room for common sense, and even frivolity, than was the case with the Italianate poems.

Some of Espinel's best poetry is to be found in this return to the older, native tradition. In the shorter line he achieves a natural, unforced flow well illustrated in the marvelous "Endechas" ("Dirge"; 187–89) in which Espinel makes use of the minor *redondillas* (see Section IV) to lament the loss of his lady's favor. There is a simple dignity to the lines which contrasts with the straining after effect found in some of his *canciones* and elegies. In the *espinelas* "No hay bien que del mal me guarde" ("There is no good which can save me from evil"; 172–74) the poet illustrates his complaint about the wrong done to him by his lady with homely examples concerning mad dogs that bite their masters and proverbs which talk of "throwing good money after bad" ("echar la soga tras el caldero"; 173) and "not touching things with a bargepole" ("De esta agua no beberé"; 173). There is a similar liveliness about "Mil veces voy a hablar" ("A thousand times do I approach"; 194–95) with its slightly varied repetitions of: "But it's better to keep quiet/ So as not to expect/ Her to send me away and good riddance". The use of the form *noramala* ("good riddance") helps to give the flavor of popular speech to this simple but effective song. Occasionally, however, the poet over-reaches himself and the result, in "Ya no más por no ver más" ("No more to see no more"; 185–87), is a *tour de force* which founders on the search for acute rhymes ("Bras," "Barrabás," "Tomás," "compás," etc.) which becomes unintentionally funny. Nevertheless, in general, the level of these "Castilian verses" is well maintained, and they have not received the critical attention which they deserve.

This other voice of Espinel speaks of love in a less anguished tone and often seeks to amuse the ladies. In a couple of glosses which are to be found earlier in the collection, the poet points to the folly of being too timid or too jealous. As he repeats in "Siempre alcanza lo que quiere" ("He always gets what he wants"; 126–27): "The man who isn't pushing/ Dies a fool and a coward"; as for jealousy, in "Pedir celos no es cordura" ("Asking for grounds for jealousy is not good sense"; 127), Espinel shows himself to be in favor of giving women freedom and letting them look after their own reputation. Similarly, in these songs, the poet does not brood on imagined slights but indulges in witty conceits, comparing his lady's favor to a lemon (183–84) or musing on the advantages of being able to talk of one's love, without revealing the lady's name — especially if you are courting two at the same time (189–90). Even a lady's tears, in this popular vein of poetry, become the subject of graceful five-line stanzas (*quintillas*), full of dewdrops, pearls, roses, and sunshine (184–85). The lover is less groveling than the Petrarchan Liseo, warning the beloved in "Si parece gran rigor" ("If it seems a great harshness"; 167–69) that, if she does not watch out, the fertile field of his love will revert to growing wild poppies. "Volved pensamiento mío" ("Recover, thoughts of mine"; 169–71) finds the poet paying back disdain with disdain and talking to his lady like a brother or a father. Espinel can now talk of favor, hope, and reward without seeing the lady's frown as the end of the world. The conceits are still there: love as a prison, for instance, in "Tiempo turbado y perdido" ("Time of upset and loss"; 180–81); so are the paradoxes, as the first line of "Ved en qué extremo me veo" ("See in what extremes I find myself"; 191–92) hints; antitheses are still used to express the lover's dilemma, as in the repeated "with" and "without" of "Sin vos y con mi cuidado" ("Without you and with my cares"; 193–94) and the "open"-"closed", "alive"-"dead" oppositions of "¿Qué me queda que esperar?" ("What is left for me to hope for?"; 174–75).

The ideal of love, however, in these poems in traditional meters is definable and attainable. It was enjoyed once, briefly, by Liseo and Célida in the Horatian idyll described in the "Eclogue to Don Hernando de Toledo the Uncle" (104–16) before slander ruined their Platonic union; it is represented in the popular poems by the oneness of Alcida and Bras in the gloss "Silvano, aunque ves, que son [Dos cuerpos]" ("Silvano, though you can see they are [Two bodies]"; 181–82). If the perfection of their relationship cannot be achieved by others, then the poet finds consolation in a more philosophical, more stoical approach to life than is possible amid the torments of Petrarchan love. The technique of the gloss lends itself to contemplative exegesis and in "Ya no quiero más placer" ("I no longer want any more pleasure"; 171–72), for example, the poet sees the imperfect delights of this life in a disabused light and becomes weary of pursuing them and, as in "Contentamientos pasados" ("Past joys"; 178–79), weary too of being haunted by the memory of what has been. Some of the glosses in this section are thus invested with, on the one hand, a sensible, even lighthearted approach to love and, on the other, a vision tinged with "claros desengaños" ("clear disillusion"; 174) which combine to give the verses in traditional meters a less exaggerated, less artificial atmosphere than the Italianate poems. This is Espinel's other voice, singing in an older tradition, rather like an Italian tenor switching from the arias of grand opera to the songs of his native Naples. The techniques and the artifice are still there but are employed in the service of a popular form and often achieve in the simpler idiom effects which are lost among the ornate structures of the cultured mode.

IX *Aspects of Style*

It is difficult in a general study of this kind, intended for the nonspecialist, to analyze the poetic style of Espinel in the depth it deserves. Nevertheless, there are certain aspects of the internal structuring and language of his poems which help to explain the special attraction which his elegant and yet straightforward diction has had for critics over the years.[10] Some of these features may be regarded as pointing the way to *Marcos de Obregón*, long regarded as a model of seventeenth-century prose.

In his love poetry, Espinel has certain affinities with Garcilaso and Herrera. In the eclogues and bucolic episodes and in the use of Italianate meters, for example, the author of *Miscellaneous Verse* might be said to be following the tradition associated with the name of Garcilaso, as did many of the poets of the sixteenth century. Dorothy Clotelle Clarke, however, has found particular echoes of Garcilaso's First and Second Eclogues in the "Egloga a Ottavio Gonzaga" ("Eclogue to Ottavio Gonzaga") and in the "Egloga Liseo," ("Liseo Eclogue") especially in respect of strophic patterns and of reminiscences of Horace's "Beatus ille." Espinel's admiration for Herrera is reflected in a penchant for colors and in the use of antitheses, particularly those of fire and ice, joy and grief, and peace and war, to express the paradox of the Petrarchan lover's situation. Thus, in the opening sonnet sequence "Vermilion in patches was appearing" (48–49), he combines vermilion, dark grey, blue, white, and bright yellow to describe the sunset which is put to shame by the beloved's arrival; "Daring, I am full of fear, I am frozen and yet burn" (45) is a succession of antitheses, related to division among the elements, to describe the bewilderment of the poet as he first feels the effects of love. Anaphora, by its use in listing the components of conflicting emotions, serves also to emphasize the tensions of love as the poet, in "En esta cárcel tenebrosa y dura" ("In this gloomy and harsh prison"; 48), sees himself: "Without happiness, without glory, without bounty and life". The lover is seen as a victim of blind Fortune, and the harshness of the beloved and words associated with these two perverse influences are a feature of the vocabulary of the love poems.

Most of these traits are common property, part of the legacy of Ovid, Horace, and Virgil and transmitted through Petrarch; or else they are part of every poet's stock-in-trade. What gives some of them added interest, in the case of Espinel, is that they match known aspects of his background and temperament and can be seen reflected later in the style of *Marcos de Obregón* (see Chapter 3, Section XII). In such a category are: the attachment to Horatian concepts; the liking for antitheses and anaphora as a means of expressing the violent extremes of his temperament; the emphasis upon colors in description; the feeling of not having received his just deserts, as expressed in vocabulary associated with hostile forces operating in the writer's life (Fate, Fortune, envy, warring elements, etc.).

In what we have referred to as Espinel's "other voice" (see Section VIII of this chapter), the poems in traditional meters have, at their best, a directness and simplicity of syntax and vocabulary, with a sprinkling of popular expressions and proverbs, which recall the lyrics of Lope de Vega. The avoidance of complicated structures and learned vocabulary, the sparing use of such poetic devices as enjambement and the freedom from poetic license and idiosyncracy in the counting of syllables are all stylistic signs which point to the fact that the short-line glosses were intended to be sung. The *canciones* too, as the name implies, may well have been given musical settings. The stress upon the musical associations of "Tender sapling, new and fertile plant" (49–51), with its "most sweet harmony" (50), its musical instruments, and the "clear voice" (50) of the beloved, reinforces this view. It was almost certainly the case with "Break the veins of the passionate breast" (106–109), which is the lament inserted into the "Eclogue to Don Hernando de Toledo the Uncle" and already commented upon in Section VI of this chapter. It is noticeable that, just before Liseo begins his complaint, Espinel illustrates his fondness for using musical terms and comparisons in passages of description. He depicts a choir of birds accompanying the song of the nightingale, with the goldfinch trilling away and the lark indulging in vibrato passages while the nightingale itself sings a descant. It is a charming picture and a concert to set the woods ringing with "sweet harmony" (106), a harmony which reinforces the Horatian idea of the blessedness of the peace and calm of the countryside. Given Espinel's fame and quality as a musician, it is hardly surprising that he should bring these predilections to bear upon the style and imagery of his poetry. As we shall see in a later chapter, this use of the world of music to illuminate a description and underline the harmoniousness of the universe is also a distinctive feature of *Marcos de Obregón*.

Espinel's talent for description is often remarked upon as part of his special charm as a Golden Age writer. In his poetry, he explores a variety of possibilities: in personal description, he ranges from the set piece which aims to capture the beauty of Cecilia de Medici in

terms of the Renaissance canon (133–35) or the hands of the beloved, all "white ivory", "transparent crystal", "snowy" and "pure"
(46–47), to the satirical self-portrait offered to amuse the Marquis of
Peñafiel (161); in a natural setting, he evokes the colors of dawn (63)
or the calm after a storm at sea (67); he can set out to impress a
patron with an extended account of the horrors of an explosion at a
powder factory (157–60) or pay tribute to the ransoming activities of
a Mercedarian friend by depicting the agonies of captivity (152–55);
from the depths of his despair at his mother's death, he paints a
portrait of himself, "yellow and pale of face" (149), as he wanders
moaning round cemeteries "turning over the white bones of the
dead" (149). On occasion, Espinel's use of natural description to
symbolize the state of mind of the lover is in the Petrarchan manner
of Herrera as with the "deserted and dry shore" of the lover's hopes,
smashed by the first line of "El aspereza, que el rigor del cielo"
("The harshness, which the severity of heaven"; 60–63). In general,
however, the range and incidence of descriptive passages in Espinel's poetry are characteristic of his own ideas and a pointer to
Marcos de Obregón.

Nowhere is Espinel's descriptive power more evident than in the
often-ignored first canto of "The House of Memory" (78–85). Critics
have been so interested in Espinel's catalogue of the men of arms
and letters of his day that they have virtually ignored the first part of
the most ambitious poem in *Miscellaneous Verse.* In it, in cadences
which have a majestic and awesome ring, Espinel makes masterly
use of the octave form to describe a journey in the imagination to the
house where Memory dwells. Memory is pictured as a Celesti-
nesque hag, "grave of aspect, severe of voice" (80), who whisks the
poet over the natural and architectural wonders of her domain and
explains to him their significance. We are reminded of the allegorical explanation of the *Cárcel de Amor (Prison of Love)* of Diego de
San Pedro or the Temple of Felicia in the *Diana* of Montemayor. In
addition to evidence of Espinel's descriptive powers, the first canto
of "The House of Memory" also offers to the reader of Espinel's
other book, the *Marcos de Obregón,* a clue to the importance and
function of memory in that work: its role in preserving things from
the ravages of Time, Death, and Fortune; its function as a "Watchtower" (81) on the world; the allegorical presentation of the rivers of
bitter and sweet water representing failure and accomplishment
(82); the recording "Of the things which in a year, a month or a day/

Happened in the world in former days" (83). The allegory surrounding Memory and her estates gives an added dimension to the description; it is also a stylistic feature which anticipates an important aspect of Espinel's other work.

One final element of the style of *Miscellaneous Verse* is the frequency with which the first person pronouns and verb-forms occur. When we are dealing with the poet as lover, this egocentricity could not be said to distinguish Espinel from other poets of the sixteenth century. It is a different matter, however, in those poems which are used to chart the stages of Espinel's personal life: the return to Ronda, the envy and provincialism of his home town, the search for patronage and escape, the confession of the excesses of youth, the travels, the failure to achieve ambitions, the temperamental shortcomings. In this aspect of his poetry Espinel comes close to that fusion of life and literary creation which is part of the secret of the vitality and fecundity of Lope de Vega. It is through the operation of the process by which life is transmuted into art in a more unstudied, instinctive way than was generally the case at the time that *Miscellaneous Verse* becomes what we have called a "poetic confession" (see Section V of this chapter), and Marcos de Obregón becomes the *alter ego* of Vicente Espinel.

CHAPTER 3

Aspects of Marcos de Obregón

I Marcos de Obregón *and the Picaresque Genre*

UNLIKE the other types of prose fiction popular in the Golden
Age, such as the sentimental, chivalresque, pastoral, Byzantine, and Moorish novels, the picaresque genre is difficult to charac-
terize. From the slyly ironical prototype, *Lazarillo de Tormes*,
through the moralistic *Guzmán de Alfarache* to the witty, de-
humanized projection of the *Buscón (The Sharper)*, each example of
the genre differs from the last, presenting a shimmering image
which has lured critics on to renewed efforts of definition in order to
accommodate them all. Some scholars have insisted that *Guzmán de
Alfarache* is the only true picaresque novel; others, in their search
for further representatives, have embraced works whose only
picaresque features have been a few minor characters, an episode or
two, or a satirical view of society. *Marcos de Obregón* has fallen into
this latter category, classified as picaresque largely because there
was no other body of fiction to which it could conveniently be attached and because certain parts of the work have a picaresque
flavor.[1]

If we apply the criteria listed by Alberto del Monte, however, we
can see that to define *Marcos de Obregón* merely as a picaresque
novel is to fail fully to appreciate its aims and qualities, and to
misjudge the artistic process whereby the author projects his aims
and ideas onto his protagonist. According to del Monte,[2] the
picaresque genre incorporates the following aspects and motifs: (1)
the pseudo-autobiographical form; (2) the genealogy of the *pícaro;*
(3) his immersion in a chaotic and deceitful world dominated by a
hostile Fortune; (4) the isolation of the *pícaro;* (5) his passage from
innocence to ill-intentioned guile; (6) his biased, polemical, and
sarcastic vision of the world; (7) the purely physical concept of exis-

tence; (8) the rogue's rejection of poverty, his desire to climb the social ladder, his struggle against Fortune — hence his egoism and lack of sensitivity, his adoption of a variety of guises, his capacity for deception, and his different ways of making a living (the latter characteristics producing wanderings from one adventure to the next, even when the *pícaro* is not presented as a *mozo de muchos amos* ["a lad of many masters"]); (9) the contrast between appearances and reality and the consequent rejection by the protagonist of honor seen as the opinion of others; (10) the condemnation of the corruption of the representatives of various levels of society, a corruption with which the *pícaro* conforms and either profits by or is deceived; (11) his final flight from reality which, as distinct from what happens in the *Lazarillo*, is generally the flight of a deserter and therefore a defeat.

Judged by this yardstick, Marcos cannot be called an anti-hero in the picaresque sense. The pseudo-autobiographical stance, in his case, is a means of fictionalizing the life of the author himself. Marcos' parentage, insofar as it is mentioned at all, is characterized by genteel poverty and respectability. When he leaves home to take up his studies and embark upon his travels, it is not with any feeling of being oppressed by a hostile world. His references to the harshness of Fortune are more routine outbursts against ill-luck than expressions of a feeling of persecution by a blind Fate. By nature gregarious, Marcos may occasionally be forced to travel alone, but he is happiest when he has someone to share good talk with and to teach. Though he may indulge in picaresque tricks, they are usually directed to the righting of wrongs. As Zamora Vicente observes: "He not only does not sin; he does not allow others to sin."[3] Marcos' view of the world is traditionalist. His disillusion is a properly Christian and positive view with its sights firmly set upon eternity, free from sarcasm and based upon traditional values of truth, honor, and religious faith. There is a spiritual dimension to Marcos' philosophy which makes the occasional descent into the scatological (vomit, excrement, etc.) seem a gratuitous concession to popular taste. Like the *pícaros*, Marcos wanders from place to place and becomes involved in a variety of adventures; there is also, from time to time, a feeling that his talents have not been properly recognized. This does not lead, however, to posing as an aristocrat, as in the case of Quevedo's Pablos or Guzmán de Alfarache, the eponymous protagonist of Mateo Alemán's picaresque novel, or to the feeling that we have in the anonymous *Lazarillo de Tormes* that the central character is being driven on by hunger. Marcos may, from time to time, cry out at the gulf which exists between human pretensions and the realities of greed and self-seeking, but it is always within a conventional patriotic and religious framework. His attitude toward honor, for example, lacks the corrosive bite of the truly picaresque view and is geared to a more humane treatment of women, as appears also in Cervantes and Tirso de Molina.[4] It is part of his conformist view of the established order whose occasional corruption, in matters of justice, for example, should not blind us to its fundamental stability. There is, therefore, no need for Marcos, at the end, cynically to become the complaisant husband, like Lazarillo, closing his eyes to his wife's misdemeanors because of the material advantages which accrue; nor does he need to seek to escape to the New World like Pablos; nor does he, like Guzmán de Alfarache, end his novelistic career as a galley slave. Marcos can quietly end his days as a charity pensioner at Santa Catalina de los Donados, secure in the knowledge that his life, though humble, has not been dedicated to self-preservation in a hostile world but rather to gathering wisdom and experience in a varied and honest career which are then to be distilled into the memoirs known by his name.

There are, of course, picaresque adventures and types scattered through the pages of *Marcos de Obregón*. The protagonist's service with the Sagredos, his student days, his return to Andalusia after his Italian trip all show signs of the influence of the "romance of roguery." Espinel's novel also shares with the picaresque genre the structural concept of a humble central character binding together a string of episodes; it shares the twin aims of entertainment and didacticism. But whereas a major contribution of the picaresque novel is the prominence given to the anti-hero as a counterblast to the idealistic fiction of the Renaissance with its noble lovers, knights-errant, and Arcadian shepherds, *Marcos de Obregón*'s blend of fact and fancy in the presentation of a hero who is humble but not rascally marks a direction in the novel which was not followed until relatively more recent times. The desire to amuse and instruct was not a prerogative of the picaresque novel but rather a Classical principle upon which that form laid particular emphasis because the Church might frown at its stress upon low-life escapades. In the case of *Marcos de Obregón*, Espinel's known admiration for Horace and the worthiness of his hero make his support of the principle of using literature to teach and entertain more readily acceptable. Insofar as *Marcos* contains passages of overt moralizing, then, of all the picaresque novels, it is closest to Alemán's *Guzmán de Alfarache*, although it must be said that Espinel is less prosy in his moralizing than the picaresque author and manages to fit his moral digressions more unobtrusively into the framework of the novel. Both authors adopt a pattern of narrative alternating with digression, but Espinel, though less stimulating, finds a more agreeable balance.

II   *Other Literary Models*

It is not difficult to find, in *Marcos de Obregón,* incidental parallels with other types of fiction popular in Spain in the seventeenth century.[5] The span of Espinel's life — 1550 to 1624 — covers also the Golden Age of the novel. Apart from the picaresque genre, all of whose major contributions fall within his lifetime, the fiction of the period mainly encompasses the pastoral, the sentimental, the chivalresque, and the Byzantine novels. Leaving aside Cervantes for the moment, these, together with the courtly short story, based upon Italian collections, and the highly colored accounts of Moorish captivity and voyages of discovery, constituted the major fare of a reading public much more limited in number than it is today. The picaresque novels, as we have seen, dealt with low-life themes, had little time for love and honor, and indulged in implicit or explicit criticism of a society seen as corrupt; idealistic fiction was escapist and aristocratic, presenting a Neo-Platonic idea of love to which the adventurers could dedicate their incredible journeys and feats of arms and the gentle shepherds, their lamentations. Since, as in the picaresque novel, this idealized view of love is entirely absent from *Marcos de Obregón,* the influence of the other types of novel and story popular at the time is likely to be tangential. The early chapters betray a knowledge of the Italian short story, and Marcos' second encounter with Dr. Sagredo leads to an account of the latter's adventures on a trip to the Straits of Magellan which owes much to the chronicles of New World voyages and to the chivalresque and Byzantine novels. Marcos' own experiences at sea have a Byzantine ring; his captivity in Algiers is a Moorish novel in miniature; and the Venetian tales of Aurelio and Camila echo similar stories from Boccaccio's *Decameron* and other Italian collections. In the main, however, the influence of the short story and idealistic fiction of the age is episodic rather than central to the thematic pattern of Marcos' account of his life. There is about *Marcos de Obregón* the tone and pace of one of the miscellanies which were also popular at the time. Typical examples were Pero Mexía's *Silva de varia lección (Miscellany of Sundry Examples)*, *El jardín de flores curiosas (The Garden of Curious Flowers)* by Antonio de Torquemada, and the *Floresta española de apotegmas y sentencias (Spanish Anthology of Maxims and Sayings)* of Melchor de Santa Cruz. These collections were intended to combine pleasant reading with a didactic function, and their method of summarizing knowledge on a wide variety of topics and illustrating conclusions with anecdotes, fables, and stories is reminiscent of Espinel's technique. The sermon collections of the day also offer a striking parallel in approach. Perhaps the closest comparison of all, this time in the realm of fiction, is with Agustín de Rojas' *El viaje entretenido (The Entertaining Journey)*[6] which, like *Marcos de Obregón*, has suffered from being categorized as a picaresque novel and then criticized for not measuring up to the criteria of that genre. In fact, it is a combination of theatre, miscellany, and sentimental novel — a fusion of elements whose popularity may be judged from the fact that seven editions were published in the twenty-five years following its first appearance. Here, in the world of fictional or encyclopedic miscellanies we are dealing with a model which is more central to Espinel's technique and approach: a key to the potpourri effect which he achieves. When it comes, however, to explaining the "hall of mirrors" effect which Espinel produces by projecting his own image on to that of his protagonist, then we must turn to Cervantes whose impact on novelistic techniques went far beyond the age for which he wrote.[7]

III *Espinel and the Critics*

Espinel's literary career spanned the middle period of the Golden Age in Spain. He belonged to the same generation as Lope de Vega, Cervantes, Mateo Alemán, and Quevedo, and even in such illustrious company his talents as a poet and musician earned him respect in the artistic milieux of the capital. Contemporary references make it clear that he exercized an influence on the rising poets of the day, representing for them a model of taste, craftsmanship, and elegance of expression which, while admitting Italianate forms, stood firm against the excesses of Gongorism. His poems were recited at meetings of literary academies, passed from hand to hand in manuscript form, and published in anthologies. His draft of *Marcos de Obregón* was similarly circulated among his friends for comment and criticism. It is curious to note that his collected poems, *Miscellaneous Verse*, while containing some interesting autobiographical items, elegant love poetry, and fulsome eulogies, can hardly bear the weight of Espinel's reputation among his contemporaries. Other factors must therefore be considered in order to account for Espinel's standing in his own day. For one thing, it is important to recognize the difference between precept and example; for another, we must allow for the rectifications of later generations of critics whose scale of values will differ from that of the Golden Age.[8] We must realize too that contemporary references to Espinel mainly take the form of *aprobaciones*, prefatory eulogies, and stanzas in long poems such as Cervantes' *Viaje del Parnaso (Journey to Parnassus)* and *Canto de Calíope (Song of Calliope)* and Lope de Vega's *Laurel de Apolo (Laurels of Apollo)* which review the poetic scene and over-praise the author's friends. There is no critical tradition, as we understand the term today. From these sources we deduce that Espinel was well-connected and held in particularly high esteem by Lope de Vega; he was a member of influential literary coteries, and from time to time enjoyed the patronage and favor of influential figures in the Church and at Court. It is possible also that his position as official book censor encouraged flattery and helped to protect him from the scurrilous attacks which were a feature of the rivalries, the jostling for favor, and the literary polemics of the day.

Recognizing the conventional nature of contemporary references and in the absence of a critical tradition, we must therefore treat with due care the encomiums of the author's friends and the conventional terminology of preliminary *aprobaciones*. *Marcos de Obregón* is unusual in having no laudatory verses as part of the preliminaries. The *aprobaciones* by the Abbot of San Bernardo, Dr. Gutierre de Cetina, and Fray Hortensio Félix Paravicino, lay the usual stress on the work's combination of moral doctrine and entertainment and on the fact that it does not offend against religion and custom. Only the famous preacher Paravicino, one of the friends who, according to the Prologue, encouraged Espinel to publish *Marcos de Obregón*, offers a brief notice of the literary qualities of the work. After the conventional statement, Paravicino commends the style, invention, and exemplary technique as befitting the pen of such a famous author. *Marcos de Obregón* seems to Paravicino the best work of its kind in Spanish. In the preliminaries to the Margarit and Cormellas editions of 1618, Luis Pujol notes the combination of serious maxims and pleasant stories. Such snippets, however, are normally of little value; they do little more than echo the formulistic phrases commonplace in Golden Age *aprobaciones*: namely, that the work satisfies the Classical precept of uniting didacticism and pleasant reading and the Inquisition requirement that it shall not contain anything contrary to the tenets of the Catholic Church or the customs and practices of the society of the day. In Espinel's case, however, it may be worth noting that the emphasis upon the Horatian formula of "prodesse et delectare" ("to give profit and delight") has a special significance given the author's acknowledgment of Horace as his master, his translation of works by the Latin poet, including the *Ars Poetica (Art of Poetry)*, and his frequent references in *Marcos de Obregón* to Horatian precepts.

Espinel's reputation seems not to have been affected when, in 1667, the *Expurgatory Index* ordered an offending paragraph to be removed from *Marcos*, a paragraph concerning a priest who said his prayers aloud while traveling (II,233–34).[9] The same notoriously blinkered *Index* ordained that an inocuous statement on charity in the *Quixote* was also offensive and condemned early editions of *Lazarillo de Tormes*, translations of Petrarch and Boccaccio, and Diego de San Pedro's *Cárcel de Amor (Prison of Love)*. To be placed on the *Index* of 1667 was, it appears, as much a mark of distinction as a condemnation.

Interest in Espinel was revived in the eighteenth century by two controversies involving his name. Tomás de Iriarte and López Sedano became involved in a dispute concerning the accuracy and value of Espinel's translation of Horace's *Ars Poetica (Art of Poetry)*.[10] López Sedano's object in including the translation in his *Parnaso español (Spanish Parnassus)* of 1768 was simply to give prominence to the first translation of the work into Castilian. Iriarte, who was preparing his own translation at the time, heaped abuse on Espinel's youthful inaccuracies in order to whip up interest in his own forthcoming version. It was a tedious and acrimonious polemic which reflected little credit on Iriarte and subjected Espinel's translation to a scrutiny it was never intended to have. The second debate arose out of the publication in 1732 of Lesage's *Gil Blas de*

Santillane and Padre Isla's attempt, through the publication of his "translation" in 1787, to restore the work to its native language.[11] Espinel's *Marcos de Obregón* proved to be a source of material for Lesage, and the debt was pointed out by Voltaire and by Padre Isla. Ironically, *Gil Blas* was widely read throughout Europe, whereas *Marcos de Obregón*, although translated into French in the same year that it first appeared in Spain, did not enjoy comparable popularity. The *Gil Blas* affair dragged on into the nineteenth century, with attempts by Llorente, Tieck, and Baret to indicate the extent of Lesage's borrowings. The balance of opinion seems to be that Lesage's scavenging was not limited to *Marcos*. Donald McGrady, for example, has recently called Lesage's work "a French adaptation of *Guzmán*, in which he omitted the 'superfluous moralizations'."[12] There is some evidence that the gentle tone of Espinel's novel, the almost bourgeois insistence on rightmindedness, the toning down of the picaresque elements were as attractive to Lesage and Neo-Classical taste as the handful of episodes which may with certainty be said to have been borrowed.

The nineteenth century saw no less than six editions of *Marcos de Obregón*, together with translations into English and German. The histories of Spanish literature of the period draw attention to the purity of the language and the tedious moralizing and make comparisons with the picaresque genre. There is, however, real progress in the attempts to fill in the details of Espinel's life. The pioneer in this area was Juan Pérez de Guzmán whose biographical sketch of Espinel appeared as a preliminary to the Barcelona edition of *Marcos* which appeared in 1881. Unfortunately, however, Pérez de Guzmán's over-literal interpretation of certain passages led to errors concerning, for example, Espinel's supposed captivity in Algiers, his service in Flanders, and his affair with Antonia Maldonado y Calatayud. These errors have been perpetuated by some modern scholars such as Gili Gaya, Calabritto, Vázquez Otero, Entrambasaguas, and Dorothy Clotelle Clarke. The appearance of the documented biography by George Haley in 1959 gave scholars the opportunity to separate fact from fiction. Haley's masterly study of the relationship between the author and his creation and the way that human experience is transmuted into artistic material within the complex temporal framework of the novel has, at last, given a European perspective to the special attraction of Espinel's work. Dorothy Clotelle Clarke's edition of *Miscellaneous Verse* was published in 1956, and María Soledad Carrasco Urgoiti's annotated edition of *Marcos de Obregón* which supplements that of Gili Gaya, in 1972. This means that modern scholarship now has the tools to probe further aspects of Espinel's elusive genius. Work has already been done on the influence of the Italian short-story writers, notably Boccaccio, on various episodes of *Marcos*, and the debt to the earlier picaresque novels has been widely recognized and studied. There are still, however, lacunae: Espinel's style, for instance, apart from his special talent for description, has not been adequately covered; nor have the directions indicated by Zamora Vicente's perceptive essay been followed up, directions which would lead to an appreciation of the philosophy behind the work and its distinctive tone and emphasis.

IV *Structure and Content*

The structure of *Marcos de Obregón* is characterized by three major features: (1) the use of interlocking time-cycles as the old protagonist reviews his early life in a series of flashbacks; (2) the interplay between fact and fiction, between the real author and the supposed author — the aged Squire — writing his memoirs; (3) the loosely-knit construction which allows the introduction of moralizing passages, digressions on a variety of topics, anecdotes involving famous contemporaries of Espinel, and novelistic episodes based upon fictional modes popular at the time.[13] The book is divided into three major sections which the author terms "relaciones" ("accounts") and each *relación* (or part) is further subdivided into chapters numbering between fourteen and twenty-six. In accordance with a fairly common practice for Golden Age prose fiction, Espinel, attempting to revitalize literary terminology, calls his chapters "descansos," a term which has been variously interpreted as "pause," "respite," or "stage."[14]

Marcos de Obregón is spending the last years of his life as a charity pensioner in Santa Catalina de los Donados, a retreat for the aged on the outskirts of Madrid. Obese and a martyr to gout, he decides to use his enforced inactivity to set down the story of his life for the pleasure and enlightenment of the public. The fictional situation thus described resembles the actual circumstances in which Vicente Espinel, as an aging, gout-ridden chapel-master decided to write *Marcos de Obregón* from his quarters adjacent to the Chapel of the Bishop of Plasencia in Madrid. The parallel thus established between the circumstances of the fictional hero and those of his creator is maintained throughout the work to lend ambivalence and an added dimension to the novelistic framework of time and space.

The novel presents a series of pictures from a life of service and travel which takes Marcos from his home in Ronda to Salamanca, Málaga, Santander, Valladolid, Seville, Africa, Italy, and back to Spain at the end of his account. The blocks of time represented by these settings are to be seen as functions of the memory of the old Squire. The opening corresponds to the period when Espinel wrote the book, i.e., 1614–16. The account begins *in medias res*, a fashionable novelistic device, with a portrait of Marcos practicing his skills as a sort of faith healer (*ensalmador*) and reminiscing about an earlier period of service with Dr. Sagredo and his haughty and foolish wife, Doña Mergelina de Aybar. The first eight chapters thus represent the gradual delineation of the protagonist and the establishment of his relationship with the parallel life and temperament of the author, woven into the fabric of Marcos' service with the Sagredos and his brief encounter with a miserly gentleman looking for a tutor for his sons. With the Sagredos, Marcos acts as counsellor to the wife and saves her from discovery when, in a lively series of scenes reminiscent of the popular one-act *entremeses* or of the Italianate short story, she becomes infatuated with a barber's boy. Although there are discrepancies in the chronology, it is clear that the first flashback is intended to be set in the 1580's.

The central section of the novel, which takes us to the middle of the third *relación*, represents a second flashback which tells the story of the early life of Marcos from the time when he received his basic schooling in Ronda until his encounter with the Sagredos and the *hidalgo*. This flashback, which covers his university days in Salamanca, his travels in Spain, his captivity in Algiers, and his adventures in Italy, together with his subsequent return to his homeland, is narrated over the period of a couple of days to a hermit in whose retreat, just outside Madrid, Marcos has taken refuge from a storm. This central block of reminiscence, which is really the heart of the book, takes us back from about 1584, when Marcos meets the hermit, to the decades between the 1550's and the 1580's, offering us scenes from Marcos' life over this thirty-year span. In it, we switch from the notion of written memoirs to the illusion of a spoken account — memories evoked in conversation with a former acquaintance to while away the time until the storm abates.

In the first part of the account, prominence is given to picaresque incidents from Marcos' travels: tricks practiced by and upon the Squire in wayside inns, encounters with rascally muleteers and gypsies, macabre scenes and curious anecdotes involving animals. At the end of the first *relación*, Marcos settles down for a while in the service of the Count of Lemos in Valladolid where, because of his ingenuity and resourcefulness, he gains a reputation as a magician.

The second *relación*, which begins on the following day in the roadside sanctuary, brings Marcos to pit his wits against the bullies and corrupt policemen of Seville before setting sail for Italy, only to fall into the hands of pirates. This gives rise to an intercalated Moorish novel, almost *de rigueur* in this kind of episodic idealistic fiction, in which the Squire's ingenuity and faith win him freedom and converts to Catholicism. The scene then changes to Italy where there is a return, as we move into the third *relación*, to the pattern of travel adventures and anecdotes coupled with an interpolated story and an episode based respectively upon typical Italian stories of revenge and deception. On his return to Madrid, Marcos falls victim to idleness and gout in the service of a noble. Wrongfully arrested, he lands in prison where he outwits a bully. It is on his release from jail that Marcos enters the service of the Sagredos, at which point he must be presumed to have left the company of the hermit.

The final thirteen chapters are dedicated to the tying up of loose ends by a series of fortuitous reunions and to the recounting by Marcos' former master, Dr. Sagredo, of fantastic adventures on land and sea on an expedition to the Straits of Magellan. The chance meetings occur on Marcos' trip back to Ronda in the mid-1580's; Dr. Sagredo's voyage, although the preparations for it faithfully echo those of the historical account of the embarkation of the fleet led by Flores de Valdés in 1581, must be assumed to take place in 1584–85, i.e., after Marcos had left their service. It is only in the last two short chapters that we see a return to Marcos as narrator as he prepares his soul for death and briefly outlines the aims and philosophy behind his memoirs.

The period covered by these reminiscences is thus roughly 1550–1614, that is to say, the lifespan of the real author, Vicente Espinel, up to the time when he began to write *Marcos de Obregón*. It should be pointed out, however, that the last twenty-five years are sketchily summarized, although the gap is to some extent filled by a network of cross-references between the time represented by the action and the later experiences of the author, a process which

strengthens the impression of the wisdom of old age being brought
to bear upon the follies of youth. This retrospective view helps to
give the work a special attraction. The book is presented as a series
of recollections from the past, chosen for their didactic and entertainment value. Like any human memory, Marcos' plays tricks with
the chronology of a life, transposing events and periods, lingering
over the episodes which the protagonist considers noteworthy while
passing hastily over times when his career seemed to be in the
doldrums.

Furthermore, behind the people, places, and happenings of the
novel, the reader discerns the figure of Espinel, directing the actions and thoughts of a character intended as an *alter ego* and oscil-
lating between the "then" and "there" of his hero's account and the
"here" and "now" of Espinel's life in Madrid at the time of writing.
The true author plays an identity game with his reader to add depth
and perspective to the narrative.

Interwoven into this account of the events of, as it were, a double
life, Marcos-Espinel offers the reader a moral commentary, the dis-
tillation of the experience of a lifetime, together with a series of
disquisitions on musical theory, medical practices, education, etc.,
and anecdotes and incidents from the lives of famous contemporaries. As a novelist commited to enlighten, entertain, and imitate the variety that is in Nature, Espinel also spices his narrative
with episodes, mainly literary in origin, which cater to the taste and
fashion of his day rather than arising out of lived experience. Each
relación contains at least one such sequence; the first has the
episodes concerning Marcos' service with the Sagredos which are
based upon the Italian short story; the second has a Moorish insert
dealing with Marcos' capitivity in Algiers; the third has Venetian
tales woven into Marcos' experiences in Italy and, in addition, six
chapters in which the Sagredos' journey to the New World is given a
treatment which is a combination of explorer's account and Byzantine novel.

These then are the structural and narrative elements which need
to be considered in detail if we are to appreciate the qualities of
Marcos de Obregón. Espinel establishes interlocking time-scales
which are interesting because of the interplay of factors within the
complicated frame of reference. He plays tricks with these time-
scales and with the relationship between author, creation, and
reader. Although his experiments do not always succeed and Es-

pinel does not always remain faithful to his master plan, the structures he attempts to use go beyond the story-telling techniques adopted by the novelists of the day and bear comparison with the layers of "reality" established by Cervantes in the *Quixote* to give depth to his novel and to establish a closer identification on the part of the reader with the act of artistic creation and with the verisimilitude of his fictional world.

On the surface of Espinel's novel, the reader is entertained by the wide-ranging adventures of Marcos in his journey through life — adventures in which Marcos alternates between protagonist and observer, narrator and listener, as the author takes us over land and sea, through picaresque incidents and tragic episodes, Italianate, chivalresque, and Byzantine encounters, intermingled with moral comments, observations on contemporary *moeurs,* and praise of the wit and wisdom of famous men of his day. This novelistic potpourri does, however, have a serious purpose hidden under the surface, as Espinel explains in his Prologue. The reader learns from the book's triumphs and disasters to admire the protagonist's resilience and fortitude. Marcos' capacity to come up smiling, if a little wryly, at the vicissitudes of the human condition is the keynote of his character. Espinel draws our attention to the importance of a stoical acceptance of unpleasantness at the beginning of the novel; again at the end he gives examples of contemporary figures whom he admires for their *paciencia.* The novel has thus come full circle. Marcos is back to the time and place of writing his memoirs at Santa Catalina de los Donados. The adventures and tribulations of his early life have been set down for posterity, and in re-living his memories, he has returned to that same virtue of forbearance with which he began his account. It is the virtue which Espinel himself perhaps conspicuously lacked in the days when he was seeking preferment in the Church after his return to Ronda. Viewed in this light, the novel thus takes on what Marichal, in another context, calls a "penitential" aspect.[15]

V *The Aims of* Marcos de Obregón

In what is commonly termed the "realistic" fiction of the Golden Age, it was usual for the author, in his prologue, to invite the discerning reader to look beneath the surface of the narrative for the hidden "fruit." There was, in other words, a moral lesson to be learned from a work whose primary purpose seemed to be to entertain. The idea of the dual function of literature — instruction and pleasure — goes back to the Classical preceptists, notably Aristotle and Horace, and was influential in the development of allegory and the exemplary tale in the Middle Ages in Spain. The early Renaissance saw a change of emphasis, the educative function of literature being seen as secondary to the pursuit of beauty. From the middle of the sixteenth century, however, the arts in Spain were considerably affected by Counter Reformational zeal. Some of the pronouncements of the Council of Trent (1545–63) were specifically concerned with artistic matters. The tendency was to deny the exclusively aesthetic appeal of the arts, enlisting it in the service of Catholicism. The effect of the reinforcement of this principle in literature and the fine arts in Spain was profound. Devotional writing, the religious treatment of secular subjects (known as *a lo divino* versions), and the painting of sacred subjects were increasingly cultivated. In imaginative literature, the didactic aspect was emphasized in titles, preliminary matter, and within the texts themselves; censors, like Espinel, further stressed the point in their *aprobaciones*. When Lope de Vega, in the opening of his *Novelas a Marcia Leonarda (Stories for Marcia Leonarda)*, states that his purpose is simply to entertain, he seems to be mocking tradition. This does not mean, of course, that from the mid-1600's Spanish literature becomes more uplifting. In the realm of the short story based on Italian models and in the picaresque novel, authors were often accused of justifying their licentiousness by paying lip service to the moral and doctrinary concept. Picaresque novelists were at pains to stress the value of teaching by negative example, urging the reader to probe beneath the surface of the narrative and including sometimes extensive moralizing passages, lest they be condemned for purveying lubricity.

Espinel, who served the Vicar of Madrid as a book censor for the Inquisition from about 1609 until the end of his career, was well aware of this climate of opinion. His opinions on literary matters were much sought after, and he was a respected member of the leading literary academies. His *aprobaciones*, over a period of twenty-five years, allowing for the encomiastic and routine nature of such statements, indicate the aims which he himself pursued in writing *Marcos de Obregón*, which he must have regarded as an example of what he had been advocating and approving over the years. The principles enunciated in these imprimaturs are a mixture of Inquisition requirements and Classical precepts as interpreted by Renaissance literary theorists: a work of literature should not go against religion and custom; it should be so well-proportioned that its episodes are seen to be relevant to the general theme; the rule concerning literary decorum should be observed so that the style is appropriate to the subject; clarity of expression should underline the exemplary nature of works of literature; the pursuit of novelty is desirable provided that it does not offend against the principles previously listed. This is a résumé of Espinel's *aprobaciones* over a period of years.[16]

One fundamental aspect, however, has so far been omitted as being worthy of separate mention. It is hinted at in the Counter Reformational tone which Espinel adopts in one or two of his imprimaturs when he commends a work for teaching a healthy and Catholic disillusion concerning the values of this world. It is clear from these *aprobaciones* and from repeated assertions in *Marcos de Obregón* that Espinel is an Establishment figure whose philosophy of life and aims in literature fit in perfectly with a Counter Reformational interpretation of the Horatian precept of combining didacticism with entertainment.[17] Espinel, in his young days, had translated some of Horace's poems and his *Ars Poetica (Art of Poetry)*; he refers to the Latin poet as "my master"; he quotes him and refers to his tenets on many occasions in his *aprobaciones* and in *Marcos de Obregón*. The dual aim of moral profit and aesthetic delight means more, however, than sugaring a didactic pill with literary ornament. The purpose behind a work of literature encompasses both the subject matter and the author's intentions in writing it so that the artist will rise to the challenge of the theme and, by his skill, give the reader a delight which is, at one and the same time, a response to the "truthfulness" of the subject and to the aesthetically satisfying, harmonious ordering of the parts of which it is composed. The combination of instruction and delight is thus a more subtle process than might at first appear, and it involves other Classical and Renaissance literary precepts. The principle of literary decorum, for example, reflects a desire for harmony and a belief in a divinely ordered universe; it is a controlling influence in achieving the Horatian aim of profit and delight. The imitation of Nature, an oft-repeated literary aim during the Renaissance, is also involved in the pleasing revelation of truth implied by "prodesse et delectare" ("to give profit and delight") as the artist seeks to echo and bring out the order and variety that is in Nature.

When we consider *Marcos de Obregón*, it is obvious that, in emphasizing the central precept of "deleitar enseñando" ("to delight by teaching") in his *aprobaciones*, Espinel was not just paying lip service to fashion but rather reiterating his own conviction that the Horatian principle held a key position in literary theory. At the beginning of the second *relación*, before going on to give an account of his experiences in Seville, Marcos outlines the aims of literature in a passage which is worth quoting in full because it constitutes an article of faith:

Books for publication should embody doctrine and pleasure to teach and delight and the ones which display no talent for this, since they do not achieve it, let them not be surreptitiously issued to make mock and offend men of esteem, or rather let them not be written at all; everything should not consist of sword-dances for, once they have been performed, no fruit is left behind, no memory of anything which clings to the soul. Books which are to be published should contain great purity and chasteness of language; purity in the choice of words and in the decency of concepts and chasteness in not intermingling irrelevancies which are foreign to the subject. . . . (II, 17–18)

Espinel stresses this aim in other passages in *Marcos de Obregón*, coupling it with a desire for "simple and clear language" (II, 308) and a plea to look beneath the surface for the hidden message of an apparently commonplace action:

It seems that with these trivial matters one is setting aside the intention contained in this account; but, if one looks closely, there is embodied a great deal of relevance to that very purpose, for here it is not the deeds of nobles and brave generals that are recorded but rather the life of a poor Squire who has to undergo these and similar things. (I, 268–69)

Marcos' Prologue perhaps puts it most succinctly: "My intention was to see if I could manage to write in prose something which might be of advantage to my country, by delighting and teaching, in accordance with that piece of advice of my master Horace . . ." (I, 32–33). Some works have erred, the Squire goes on, in the direction of an excess of moral doctrine; others have concentrated too much on jocular material. The secret is to find the right balance: "morality has room for delight and delight space for doctrine, because virtue — if one scrutinizes it closely — holds great pleasure for the one who espouses it and delight and entertainment offer plenty of opportunity for consideration of the purpose of things" (I,33).

It is clear, therefore, that in composing *Marcos de Obregón* Espinel saw the Horatian precept of delight combined with moral profit as central to his purpose and as containing within it, as it were, other Classical and Renaissance literary principles. His subject matter — the humble doings of a Squire — lent itself to a retrospective treatment which could, in its turn, be used to emphasize virtue, wisdom, and patience. In the ordering of the parts, Espinel could satisfy the demand for relevance, decorum, and the imitation of the harmony and variety of Nature. Thus, the truthfulness of Espinel's narrative is morally and aesthetically satisfying in terms of Renaissance literary theory. His Squire's activities are decorous, in the sense that they are confined to largely everyday incidents rather than the world of great deeds; the variety provided by the combination of episode, digression, moralizing, and anecdote is unified by the presentation of the character and aspirations of Marcos as an *alter ego* of Espinel. The pace is leisurely, reminiscent of the tone and texture of Cervantes' *Don Quixote*. Cervantes, echoing Renaissance preceptists such as López Pinciano, envisaged the novel as a "wide and spacious field" (*DQ*,III,350), "a cloth woven of various strands" (*DQ*,III,351), reflecting the variety of Nature itself; Espinel, in *Miscellaneous Verse*, quotes with approval the Italian dictum: "Per troppo variar' natura è bella" ("Nature is beautiful because of its many variations"; 162).

There is, however, one further aspect of the aims of *Marcos de Obregón* which needs to be elucidated in the light of Neo-Aristotelian literary theory. It is hinted at in the continuation of a quotation already used, taken from the final chapter:

I wrote it in simple and clear language, in order not to give the reader trouble understanding it. Master Valdivielso, with the vividness and clarity of his sharp mind, expressed it very well when he said to a poet who prides himself on writing in a very obscure fashion that if the object of History and Poetry is to delight by teaching and to teach by delighting, how can what is incomprehensible, or at least what must give the reader great trouble in understanding, teach and delight? (II,308).[18]

Here, the Aristotelian distinction between history and poetry is coupled with Espinel's central Classical concept of the didactic and aesthetic functions of literature and with the belief in clarity of expression. The relevance to *Marcos de Obregón* is that, in Aristotelian terms, if history is concerned with the local and particular, with facts and things that have happened, then poetry (here used in the sense of imaginative literature in general) deals with the ideal and universal, with fancy and things that might or ought to have been. It is clearly a major objective of *Marcos de Obregón*, within the general aim of combining instruction and entertainment, to bring together these two worlds of fact and fancy. In using the broad framework of his own life as the basis of Marcos' wanderings and in referring to people he knew, places he had visited, events he had witnessed, Espinel is using the historian's approach, to use the term in an Aristotelian sense; in weaving stock types and episodes into the fabric of the narrative, Espinel is employing the standard methods of the imaginative artist. The aim is to synthesize the two activities and produce a hybrid form, a fictionalized autobiography which, while not always consistent in its objectives, represents a breakdown of the barriers between the genres erected by Classical theory; it is also a step forward in novelistic technique under the umbrella of the Horatian formula of moral uplift combined with aesthetic pleasure.

VI   Marcos de Obregón *as Autobiography*

Marcos de Obregón is a curious amalgam of fact and fiction or, to express it in the Neo-Aristotelian literary terminology current in the Golden Age, of History and Poetry. The subtitle of George Haley's study of Espinel, *A Life and Its Literary Representation*, indicates the degree of interest which modern criticism has taken in the work as a fictionalized autobiography.[19] Various justifications for this line of approach may be advanced: there are many points of similarity between the pattern of Espinel's life, as we now know it, and the travels and experiences of Marcos; furthermore, Espinel used the novel as a frame for a gallery of portraits of his contemporaries, flattering tributes to people of taste and influence whose paths had crossed his own; the philosophy of life which retrospectively guides the thoughts and actions of the Squire belongs to the old chapel-master of the Capilla del Obispo de Plasencia, Vicente Espinel; the author also uses the autobiographical technique to produce a mirage effect in which the "I" of the narrator stands for both Marcos and Espinel, the latter being represented, in addition, as "So-and-so", "X" and "the author of this book."

The starting-point, then, is the projection of the facts of the author's life onto that of his fictional creation. Thus, Marcos and his creator are shown to have had a common birthplace, Ronda, for which they feel affection and nostalgia mixed with an awareness of its remoteness and provincialism. Author and protagonist studied at the University of Salamanca and became involved in the musical life of the city. Although the details of Espinel's travels in Spain after leaving Salamanca are not known, it is clear from references in the poetry and elsewhere that, like Marcos, he went through a period of restless wandering before leaving for Italy; equally probable is the fact that, prior to embarkation, Espinel spent some time in Seville, mirroring his hero's experience. The author's stay in Italy is well documented, and there is little doubt that, in broad outline, it coincides with Marcos' visit, especially with regard to poetic and musical activities and the adverse effect of the climate of northern Italy on the traveler's health. Running through all these experiences from the early days to the return to Madrid from Italy, there are constant reminders of the links between Espinel's life and that of his creation: references to Ronda and a common family background, to the state of health of the "author" and, in particular, his gout, and to his reputation as a musician and as a poet known for verses in Latin and Castilian.

At the same time, however, certain areas of Espinel's life do not feature in Marcos' account. Apart from passing references to a family chaplaincy in Ronda and to his entering the priesthood, Espinel makes no mention of the traumas arising from his attempts to gain preferment in the Church and from his absenteeism due to his involvement in the musical and literary life of the capital. Nor do his activities as a chapel-master or a book censor for the Inquisition feature in Marcos' life story. The Squire is made into a humbler figure than the true author, and the events between his return to Ronda and the time of writing his memoirs (i.e., roughly 1589 and 1614) are sketched out in a few lines. In effect, Marcos' story only deals with his career up to the age of about fifty. Material from the last third of the joint life of creator and creation is used anachronistically to relate the period represented by the narrative to the wisdom and experience of the aged autobiographer; it is part of the retro-spective dimension of the novel. It should also be pointed out that, if some parts of Espinel's life do not feature in *Marcos de Obregón*, other parts of Marcos' experiences are clearly literary in origin and do not arise out of lived experience. Modern research has shown that the adventures recounted in the first flashback when Marcos saves his master's wife from discovery after her affair with the barber's lad are largely based upon Boccaccio; when, at the end of his stay in Italy, Marcos hears the sad tale of Aurelio's revenge upon a supposedly erring wife and later outwits the courtesan Camila, in each case the source is the Italian short story. Many of the tricks perpetrated by and upon Marcos in his travels through Spain and Italy are reminiscent of folklore tales and episodes from the picares-que novel and from the one-act *entremeses* (humorous plays) popu-lar in Espinel's day. The novelist himself is responsible for blurring the frontiers between personal experience and imaginative writing as part of the game which he plays intermittently with the reader whom he tries to confuse as to the shifting identity of Marcos and the level of reality represented by the fictional account of his pro-tagonist's adventures. Thus, in the second Prologue, the writer gives as one of his reasons for publishing *Marcos de Obregón* the fact that "a certain gentleman" had been passing off the "short story of the tomb of San Ginés" (I,34) as his own; in the chapter in which it appears in the novel (*Relación 1, Descanso* v),[20] Marcos passes the story off as an incident in his own life and links it to a similar happening in Ronda. It is not surprising, therefore, that critics using *Marcos de Obregón* as a source for filling in the gaps in Espinel's life have produced a somewhat romanticized account. The casual men-tion of the beauty of Antonia Maldonado y Calatayud has been linked to the Célida of the love poems to produce an ill-substantiated tale of unrequited passion; the reference to Flanders and the Battle of Maestricht has been taken literally, without sup-porting evidence; the novelesque adventures of Marcos' captivity in Algiers, which constitute an interpolated Moorish novel, as was the fashion in the idealistic fiction of the day, have produced a supposed period of captivity in Espinel's life for which the known chronology does not allow. Thanks to the work of Haley, it is now possible to tread delicately through this minefield of half-truths and, by separat-ing fact from fiction, judge Espinel's achievement as a novelist.

Although there are, as we have indicated, similarities between the events of Marcos' life and that of his creator, the novel's autobiographical flavor is perhaps best captured when one looks at it as a register of the people Espinel knew and admired. It is possible to build up a picture of literary and musical gatherings in the houses of the cultured rich, of the area around the Church of San Andrés where Espinel lived and worked, of the author's attempts to build up a reputation as a poet and musician and to interest nobles with a taste for the arts in giving him support and patronage, and of that circle of literary and ecclesiastical friends and acquaintances in the capital whose company the novelist so enjoyed that it made the life of Ronda irksome. The index of the names of contemporaries mentioned by Espinel in *Marcos de Obregón* is an impressive array of talent and distinction and a fair indication of the people to be cultivated by a struggling artist in the Madrid of the beginning of the seventeenth century.[21]

Another aspect of the self-portrait contained in the work is the accuracy with which it reflects the ideals and aspirations of the true author. *Marcos de Obregón* offers us what might be termed the "spiritual biography" of Espinel, the "chain of sentiments," to use Rousseau's phrase, which makes up an artist's view of himself.[22] There is an elegiac or confessional tone to the book which is the product of age looking back upon the lost opportunities of youth and, by way of self-justification, putting a brave face on the less-than-heroic incidents of a humble life by investing them with an exemplary or didactic quality. Espinel does not indulge in wearisome moralizing passages in the manner of a Mateo Alemán to purge himself of the excesses of an Andalusian temperament; he sees himself instead, as others saw him in his old age, as a prudent, wise counsellor advising others of the dangers of life and grafting the fruits of his long experience onto the tribulations and adventures of his hero. Interwoven into the narrative are the teachings and counsel of a lifetime; ideas about education, human vices and virtues, honor, patience, all of which reflect a nobility of spirit which Espinel would have liked to have displayed throughout his long life and which sets *Marcos de Obregón* apart from the picaresque novels with which it is so often compared. Espinel, the book censor for the Inquisition, the poet, musician, and priest whose genealogy, like that of his hero, goes back to petty nobility from the region of Santander honored for their participation in the Reconquest, imbues his only prose work with a disabused serenity, a firm and calm enunciation of traditional values which marks him as a post-Tridentine Catholic, a patriot, a man of his time.

And yet the autobiographical mode is deceptive, a shimmering image. It is perhaps worth dwelling on the impossibility of the exercise by which an artist attempts to evoke the objective happenings of his own life. As Stendhal puts it: "What eye can see itself?" For the autobiographer orders, selects and interprets the data of his own life, shaping his material as a novelist might shape it to produce the result he wants. Autobiography thus becomes not the biography of a person written by himself but the biography of an imaginary person made up of vital elements taken from the character and experience of the author. The I-subject does not become the I-object but is refracted through the author's mature imagination, expressing a retrospective relationship with the past rather than historical truth. Once again, therefore, Espinel is bringing the worlds of History and Poetry together by the use of his backward-looking technique and, instead of reconstructing his life, he portrays himself in the figure of Marcos reliving his life by writing it down. He gives his other *persona* a different name, and a different life-style and, by intermingling novelistic material with the autobiographical element, produces a hybrid form which literary historians have found difficult to classify. To call *Marcos de Obregón* "memoirs" or a "fictionalized autobiography" and leave it at that is to do Espinel less than justice. The interplay between the levels of reality, the fluctuations in the point of view between Espinel and his creation have been regarded by some critics as flaws in the structure of the work; others have seen them as reflecting a typical Mannerist technique whereby the boundaries between appearance and reality, illusion and truth are explored. The truth, as usual, probably lies somewhere between the two positions. Whatever may be the flaws in implementation, the exploitation of the ambivalence by Espinel points the way to the modern novel. [23]

VII   *Time and Memory*

In Section IV of this chapter, we have already indicated the extent to which Espinel uses the flashback technique within the two inter-locking time-cycles represented in *Marcos de Obregón*. The moment of writing (1614–16), which is the first cycle, is the same for Marcos and for Espinel; the period covered by the narrative

(1550's–1616), because of the use of flashbacks, does not run consecutively, nor are the blocks of time represented within this second cycle dealt with in similar detail. In addition, there is a series of cross-references between the "here" and "now" of the simultaneous composition of Marcos' and Espinel's life story and the "then" and "there" of the incidents recounted. The process is a two-way one, superimposing upon the events the wisdom of hindsight and projecting forward from the past with a prophetic eye. As with the autobiographical aspect of *Marcos de Obregón* and the presentation of an "I" which shifts between Marcos and Espinel, the supposed and the true author, some scholars have preferred to dwell on Espinel's failure consistently to preserve the distancing demanded by this doubling of the image of the narrator; others have taken the process, "warts and all," as an exploration of the no-man's land between illusion and reality, typical of the bipolarity of thinking of the Baroque artist, or perhaps more accurately in the case of Espinel, of the transitional Mannerist approach to art. This latter point of view pays more attention to the workings of the human memory in roving over the ages of man and superimposing the experience of one upon the folly of another. It is a subject in which, in the course of the novel, Espinel himself expresses an interest (see *Relación* 3, *Descanso* xiv). Memory frees the past by associations in the present, like a wine releasing its bouquet. At the same time, memory can play tricks by juxtaposing events in the mind and by associating the wisdom of age with the often ill-considered acts of youth. These tricks of memory should not simply be labeled, as some critics have done, technical faults which illustrate Espinel's failure to maintain the vantage point he established at the outset. They also add something to richness and complexity of the work by giving it a human touch: a failure accurately to recall the sequence of incidents in a life and a tendency to be wise after the event.

At the beginning of the novel, the Squire is presented as an old man about to write his memoirs from what Mateo Alemán might have called the "watchtower" of the "last third of his life" (I,40). The situation of Espinel as he prepares to write *Marcos de Obregón* is thus linked from the outset with that of his creation and the story Marcos is to tell, from a Ronda childhood through student days in Salamanca, travels in Spain and Italy, and a return to Madrid and to his birthplace bears a striking resemblance to the main stages in the life of his creator. Marcos and Espinel start their reminiscences from

the same point, i.e., 1614–16, but the period covered by the
memoirs is not presented in chronological sequence. The first
flashback takes us back to the 1580's and acts as a preview or as a
curtain raiser to the main feature. Marcos' service with the Sagredos, which gives us the flavor of what is to follow, leads into the
second flashback when Marcos, in conversation with a hermit, reviews his life from his schooldays in Ronda in the 1550's up to the
point where he takes refuge from the storm in the hermit's *humilladero* (roadside sanctuary) after his stay with the Sagredos. The
novel then changes back from a spoken account to the written
memoirs with which it began in order to recount adventures in
Madrid, a trip to Ronda, a further meeting with Dr. Sagredo who
takes over as narrator to tell of his expedition to the New World, and
a brief outline of events up to the time of writing.

Not only is the sequence of events not consecutive, it also covers
only part of the narrator's life in any sort of detail. The period
between 1589 — the date of Marcos' return trip to Madrid and of
his chance reunions with Dr. Sagredo and the children of the renegade he served in Algiers — and the time of writing the memoirs
(1614–16) is covered in the most cursory fashion. The reason for this
is hinted at in the author's cryptic reference to a change of vocation
(II,257). In retrospect, Espinel — not Marcos, to whom the remark
does not apply — can see that his entry into the priesthood, which
can be set in the late 1580's, was a watershed in his life. He prefers
not to talk about the storms of his years as a priest in Ronda and of
the reputation for asperity and backsliding which he gained as a
result. It is not until he has settled in Madrid as a chapel-master and
established himself as a respected poet and musician that he can
contemplate novelizing his memoirs. Even then, he exercizes his
privilege as creator of the fictional world of Marcos by selecting the
material to be used, giving it a patina of the wisdom which comes
only from age and experience and manipulating the time-sequence
of his account in accordance with the accepted practices of the
idealistic fiction of the day. This allows him to begin *in medias res*
and, using the flashback and interpolation techniques common in
the Byzantine and pastoral novels, progress by a series of recapitula-
tions. At the end, he uses chance meetings to draw the strands of his
novel together. In Espinel's case, however, the adroit handling of
the time-scale represented by Marcos' reminiscences enables him to
draw a veil over those parts of his life which either might not lend

themselves to a novelistic treatment or might not show him in a good light. And, by so doing, he can still use the intervening period — names, places, anecdotes — as a point of reference for his earlier memories.

One further advantage of this partial account of Marcos' life as parallel to Espinel's own is that the use of data from the twenty-five-year gap in the chronology and, more particularly, from the period immediately preceding the composition of *Marcos de Obregón* illustrates the way that the human memory works. The inconsistencies concerning the protagonist's age, the superimposition of names and anecdotes from the later period upon the framework of earlier events, the apparent discursiveness, the variations in pace and in depth of treatment — all these aspects of *Marcos de Obregón* bespeak the fallibility of an old man's memory as he attempts to recapture the past and invest it with a golden glow of virtue and wisdom. The associations, illustrations, and parallels which interrupt the flow of the narrative are not the undisciplined ramblings of a tedious old bore but rather the conscious attempt by a mature artist to mirror the effect of the vagaries of memory upon the recollection of past time. Chance associations are shown liberating the memories of the past and merging them with the present. Although some critics tend to dwell on the inconsistencies of the process, pointing to Espinel's lack of coordination and control, a more fruitful approach is perhaps to see this exploitation of the artistic possibilities of time and memory as an early stage in the development of the modern novel toward the subtlety of Marcel Proust's exploration of the same territory in *A la recherche du temps perdu*. Although Espinel's rearrangement of the time-sequence might be influenced by the idealistic fiction of the day and his retrospective stance by the picaresque novel, there is an extra dimension to his use of these techniques which has not adequately been assessed by modern critics.

VIII *The Mood of the Work*

In the two prologues to *Marcos de Obregón*, Espinel and his Squire explain to their patron, the Cardinal Archbishop of Toledo, the motives which led them to publish their memoirs. Espinel vividly describes the conflicting feelings which did battle within him until he was persuaded by friends to issue his *Marcos* "empty of

virtues and full of troubles" (I,31); his protagonist emphasizes the
lessons to be learned from his experiences in facing up bravely to
the perils of time and Fortune. This combination of a lack of asser-
tiveness with a plucky attitude toward adversity offers us a clue to
the elusive charm of the work. In terms of its mood and atmosphere,
Marcos de Obregón occupies the middle ground between the
picaresque novel and the idealistic fiction of the age: it lacks both
the harshness of the former and the starry-eyed quality of the latter.
The ideals of moderation, tolerance, humility, and courtesy which it
advocates are orthodox and attainable. Marcos has a noble spirit
which no amount of masquerading by Quevedo's Pablos can
achieve, and yet he does not dedicate himself, like Amadís de
Gaula, to a life of high adventure in pursuit of an impossible ideal.

Espinel's attitude toward honor, as expressed through Marcos, is
an illustration of the difference in approach. When the Squire comments on the sad tale of Aurelio, it is to turn aside the expected,
gory dénouement. Aurelio has killed his majordomo on suspicion of
having an affair with his wife and, having murdered another servant
because he knew too much, is in the process of starving his wife to
death when Marcos encounters him. In his observations, Marcos
stresses the circumstantial nature of the evidence against the wife
and the continuing love Aurelio feels for her. Thus the harsh dic-
tates of an impersonal code of conduct, which demands her death,
are softened by an appeal to natural justice and the validity of
human emotion so that a happy ending is produced.[24] There is a
similar healthy-mindedness about the advice which Marcos offers
elsewhere in the novel. In captivity in Algiers, the Squire does not
hesitate to indoctrinate the children of the renegade in the ways of
Catholicism, and he encourages his fellow-captives to bear their
troubles with Christian fortitude; his prescription for the perfect
tutor, given to an *hidalgo* who seeks to employ him, unites wisdom
and humanity. But this orthodoxy, as we have seen in the case of
Aurelio's honor problem, gives way to common sense when rigid
adherence to principle could produce unhappiness or even tragedy.
When a repentant Doña Mergelina de Aybar, whom Marcos serves
as counselor in the first flashback sequence in the novel, regrets her
foolish affair with the barber's lad, she is lectured by the Squire on
the virtues of a discreet silence. The gentleman who comes to Marcos for advice because he cannot eat, relax, or sleep, is taken for an
invigorating walk and told to keep to a frugal diet. Thus does Marcos

temper high-mindedness with common sense, and this combination of qualities in the advice he so freely offers gives the work a pleasant, down-to-earth flavor. Solid, old-fashioned virtues are shown to be applicable, with a little adjustment to suit particular situations, to humble lives. Not a low life, like that of a *pícaro* who is a desperate social climber, nor a life dedicated to the unattainable, like that of a knight-errant or a literary shepherd, but a modest, decent life of service, like that of a Squire.

The virtue Marcos most admires is patience; the deadly sin he most fears is sloth. Time and again in the novel he praises examples of patience in others and counsels forbearance when asked for advice. The opening of the book, in which Marcos is criticized out of earshot for his activities as a quack doctor, gives rise to a series of anecdotes concerning famous contemporaries who have exhibited the virtue of patience; a parallel series brings *Marcos de Obregón* to a close. This emphasis on a tolerant acceptance of adversity gives the novel a good-humored, though sometimes self-satisfied, atmosphere. Espinel makes it clear that the patience he advocates emanates from Christian Stoicism; it has a heroic quality, akin to fortitude:

In Italy they say that patience is food for idlers; but this one understands as a vicious form of patience and the one who professes it, in order to eat, drink and enjoy his leisure, suffers indignities unimaginable among human beings. In my case, we are dealing with that patience which adorns and refines virtue and which gives security to life and to the peace of the mind and of the body. . . . (I,47)

On a couple of occasions in the novel, Marcos falls victim to the kind of sloth which, according to Espinel, the Italians recognize as a travesty of true patience, and each episode leads to near-disaster. In Seville, idleness causes him to fall victim to a braggart and he nearly lands in jail; in Madrid, after his return from Italy, he finds a comfortable niche in a noble household, becomes fat, a prey to gout and, as a result of his idle wanderings through the city, is falsely arrested and goes to prison for three months. These adversities, however, serve to halt the protagonist's decline into sloth, and his old resourcefulness and capacity for cheerful acceptance of misfortune return to sustain him.

On the face of it, therefore, the mood of *Marcos de Obregón* is an optimistic and uplifting one in which the reader is entertained and, at the same time, taught a lesson in Christian fortitude. There are, however, hints that the "secret" buried beneath the surface of the novel, to which reference is made in the Prologue, is more than just a nod in the direction of convention or a plain message concerning the patient acceptance of adversity. When, in the opening *Descanso* (or chapter), Marcos is shown as an *ensalmador* (healer) and associated with contemporary examples of patience, Marcos finishes the chapter by recounting how he came to enter the service of the Sagredos: "for after many misfortunes, which I have suffered all my life, I came to find myself stranded at the end of my old age and, in order not to be arrested as a vagabond, I had to throw myself on the mercy of a friend of mine, a chorister in the Capilla del Obispo . . ." (I,47–48). Now, Espinel is here playing the identity game with which the reader becomes familiar in the course of the work. The uncertainty over Marcos' age (he should not, in the 1580's when he entered the service of the Sagredos, remember himself as being very old) and Espinel's pose as a "friend" associated with the music of the Capilla del Obispo point to a superimposition of present on past and an ambivalence concerning the relationship between real and supposed author which are typical of Espinel's technique. At the same time, if one views the rest of the novel as stemming from this ambivalence, then the opening flashback showing Marcos triumphantly dealing with the choleric Dr. Sagredo and his haughty wife can be seen as symbolic of Espinel's conquest of his own unruly temperament by the exercise, in later life, of patience and self-control. Marcos, as Espinel's *alter ego,* nostalgically recalls a youth in which he became respected and admired for his resource and forbearance; the novelist Espinel fictionalizing his own memories, projects a plea for moderation and tolerance on to these episodes as a sort of apologia or confession for the immoderate, intolerant outbursts of his early years as a priest in Ronda. Viewed in this light, *Marcos de Obregón* acquires a subterranean penitential flavor.

Perhaps significantly, the novel does not deal, except in a most cursory fashion, with the author's entry into holy orders. A deliberate vagueness comes over the later career of Marcos, and the turbulent decade of Espinel's life, the 1590's, does not feature in Marcos' account. One cryptic reference, however, to a "prebendary friend of mine" has the flavor of true autobiography. He appears on Marcos' return to Málaga on unspecified business to do with the Cathedral.

Among the worthy priests associated with the Málaga see, Marcos singles out this one: "a man of good family, of great and superior virtues, very worthy of esteem, who was in high dudgeon because without cause men who could in no way be compared to him were taking offence at his absences" (I,222). The link with Espinel's troubles with his fellow-priests in Ronda in connection with his absenteeism seems clear enough.

This, then, is that added dimension which links the "chain of sentiments" piously avowed by Marcos to the subconscious guilt of Espinel concerning his early excesses. It gives a richness and complexity to *Marcos de Obregón*, a special quality to its nostalgia which gives the reader the feeling that, for all the tricks of the novelist's trade, he can hear beneath the surface of the work, the real, sad voice of Vicente Espinel.

IX *The Humor of* Marcos de Obregón

Humor is a much-neglected aspect of the so-called "realistic" fiction of the Golden Age, and yet there is evidence to suggest that the picaresque novels and *Don Quixote* were considered in their day primarily as funny books.[25] The modern reader, however, inevitably loses the topical flavor of many of the jokes, and he also finds that over the years tastes in humor have changed. In the drama and novel of Espinel's time, many of the funny scenes and episodes depended upon slapstick and often displayed cruel and scatological features. Judged by the yardstick of modern taste, this emphasis upon physical effects seems earthy and brutal, somewhat akin to "black" humor. Although less bawdy than the writers of Elizabethan England or of France and Italy of the same period, Spanish novelists and playwrights took the same delight in depicting pain and cruelty for humorous ends, found idiots and cripples funny, and indulged in obscene stories and jokes about vomit and excrement which have only a minority appeal today. The *pícaros,* Don Quixote and Sancho, the fools and jesters of the plays of the period all receive beatings and wallow in filth in search of a laugh.

Espinel follows the prevailing fashion in humor and involves his hero in scatological and farcical situations which depend for their effect upon a physical concept of existence. There is, however, a certain lack of gusto in his treatment, as though the scenes were a concession to popular taste. The idea that a barber's lad should cultivate the guitar in order to scratch the sores on his wrists as he plays may be genuinely funny but when he comes to the house of Doña Mergelina de Aybar smelling because someone has emptied the contents of a chamber-pot over him, Espinel uses a euphemism to describe the cause of the stench (1,ii). There are scatological episodes, too, when maggots from a hanging corpse drop on to Marcos' face as he sleeps (1,x), when he drinks his own bath-water and vomits it back (1,xi), and when he and his student companions try to burn the decomposing leg of a dead mule in mistake for a log (1,xii). These incidents, in Espinel's hands, however, seem gratuitous excursions into the physically repugnant and not part of what one critic has called the "excremental vision"[26] which symbolizes the true *pícaro's* degradation. When pranksters in the household of the Count of Lemos want to exploit Marcos' reputation as a magician and persuade a dwarf that the Squire can make him taller, it is significant that Espinel tells the tale of the midget's discomfiture and shows the Count enjoying the story but causes his hero to refuse to take part in the cruel jest and to make pious noises about not interfering with Nature (1,xxiii).

Nor does Espinel display the wit that is characteristic of Quevedo or the gentle irony and satire found in *Lazarillo de Tormes.* He is sparing in his use of puns and alliterative humor, although Marcos' contest with the compulsive talker who latches on to him as he is returning home from Salamanca (1,xviii) has a Quevedesque ring, as does the scene in the servants' hall from which Marcos makes his escape from the *hidalgo* to take shelter with the hermit (1,viii). There is also a quality of parody, again reminiscent of Quevedo, about the young rogue who turns casual conversation into a parade of witticisms (3,xv). Espinel generally chooses safe targets for his rare satirical moments: the character of the Portuguese and the Venetians (2,vi; 3,viii); Jewish ancestry (1,xxii); medical jargon and doctors (1,iv); the administration of justice (1,xii; 2,v); the foibles of village priests (1,xiii; 3,xv). The Inquisition took exception to the last of these references in the *Index* of 1667 when a passage concerning a priest who said his prayers aloud as he walked along was ordered to be cut. In general, however, Espinel is too much a supporter of orthodoxy, tradition, and the Establishment to attack the system. His comments on Marcos' brush with the authorities in Seville, for example, take the edge off any satirical intention by pious moralizing, and he uses the encounter with the chief magistrate of

Salamanca as an illustration of what can be achieved by courtesy and humility. Proof that satire is not to his liking comes in a passage from the evidence given by Espinel to Pérez Roy in his investigation of the background of Torres Rámila: ". . . the person who satirizes only does so in order to spew out his poison or show off his wit, and not so as to tell the truth and because he feels deep down what he says to be true. . . ."[27]

Espinel's humor is displayed to its best advantage in the practical jokes played by and on Marcos, in the stratagems which illustrate his resourcefulness and in farcical incidents with a strong visual element. He is good at describing scenes and people so that the comic aspect of a situation is brought out. Again, however, he takes the sting out of many of these episodes by emphasizing that practical jokes should not be played for revenge and that innocent third parties should not be harmed by them. Although this lessens the cruelty of some of the japes in which Marcos is involved, the tendency to include a moral homily at the end of them has a dampening effect on the comedy. Nevertheless, Marcos' hoaxes and tricks constitute a major source of the book's humor: his planting of the cape on the rogue who dined at his expense (1,ix); the way he diverts the merchants' gold from the grasp of the confidence tricksters (1,xiii); how he escapes from the cellar of the mistress of the thug he outsmarted in Seville and then, posing as a helpless beggar, is carried to safety by one of his pursuers (2,ii; 2,v); the discomfiture of the would-be thief, Camila (3,viii–ix); the humiliation of the prison bully when Marcos shaves off half of his luxuriant moustache (3,xii). In all these cases, Espinel is careful to justify his Squire's actions by having him pay back miscreants in their own coin. Nor does Marcos have it all his own way. His journey to and stay in Salamanca may be compared to a *pícaro*'s training in *bellaquería* ("cunning"). In the Mesón del Potro (1,ix), for example, he is duped by a rogue's flattery into paying for food and drink in the same way that Pablos and his master are tricked at the Inn of Viveros in the *Buscón (The Sharper)*.

In his travels through Spain and northern Italy and during his captivity in Algiers, Marcos earns a reputation as a sharp-witted schemer. His use of red ochre to discover a thief (1,xvi) and his unmasking of a gipsy's plot to pass off an intractable mule by doping it with wine (1,xvi) are early examples of his skill. Later, in Algiers, he devises a scheme whereby he can whisper words of love to the renegade's daughter in the guise of casting a secret spell to cure her melancholy (2,x), and, indeed, Marcos wins his freedom as a reward for a successful stratagem by which he trains a thrush to talk in order to let the King know that his own favorite is stealing from the treasury (2,xii). The Squire also secures his release from prison in Italy by deceiving his jailer into thinking that he has discovered the philosopher's stone (3,i) and later unmasks the trickery of a necromancer (3,iv).

In Marcos' *burlas* (tricks) and stratagems, the targets are generally deserving of their fate. The humorous effect is somewhat lessened by the overt moralizing which accompanies the deceptions. In one or two cases, the strong visual impact of the scene described is enough to triumph over the sanctimoniousness. This is the case with two early episodes: in the first, there is a hilarious account of Doña Mergelina's affair with the barber's lad nearly being discovered by Dr. Sagredo (1,iii); in the second, the confrontation between the proud *hidalgo* and a herd of cows on a narrow bridge ends in comic disaster (1,viii).

This brief review of the humor in *Marcos de Obregón* cannot do justice to the charm and pace of some of the episodes. It does, however, indicate the softening effect which Espinel's moral stance has on the more cruel and corrosive aspects of the comic vision of his day. There are concessions to contemporary tastes in humor by the occasional scenes which explore the physically repugnant, but in general, Espinel achieves his effects by the cleverness of his protagonist's schemes and by the visual appeal of the episodes he describes.

X   The Digressions

As with *Guzmán de Alfarache*, some critics have found the combination of narrative and digression in *Marcos de Obregón* makes for tedium and loss of concentration.[28] It is important, however, to judge any Golden Age novel against the background of Classical and Renaissance literary theory, especially in relation to the shape and purpose of a work of fiction (see Section VI of this chapter). Seen in this light, the digressions form an integral part of the interwoven tapestry of the novel, a strand which helps to give depth to the particular incidents which make up the plot by relating them to the general moral concepts and ideas which inspired the author to write the book. Obviously, the harmony of proportions in the work must be preserved or the author may be justly criticized for prolixity. The method, however, of combining a first-person narrative with reflective passages to produce a leisurely, meandering work which entertains and instructs has an impeccable ancestry.

Espinel, in his disquisitions, ranges over a wide spectrum. The topics he deals with may be conveniently divided into four categories: (1) those intended to give *Marcos de Obregón* the flavor of a miscellany, reflecting the range of interests of a man of Espinel's time; (2) matters which, while being of general application, also mirror the author's specialties; (3) subjects relating to and justifying the aims of the book; (4) "organic" and reiterated concepts which help to underline the theme of the work.

In achieving his potpourri effect, Espinel adopts an orthodox position on a number of topical issues. He joins with many Golden Age authors, for example, in repeatedly condemning the vice of gambling (1,xiii; 1,xxii; 3,xxiv); he fears for the way that justice is administered in Spain (2,v), although he is careful, in this case, to hedge his remarks around with diplomatic *caveats;* he expresses a balanced opinion on the burning question of royal favorites (2,xii). In other areas, his interests are more general: the question of human greed (3,ii); the Spaniard abroad (3,i); the wiles of women (2,iv).

Espinel's special interests are easily identifiable by the way in which certain topics recur or are dealt with in greater depth. There are three main areas in this category: medicine, music, and education. The obesity and gout which plagued the author from his mid-thirties until his death gave him an interest in the contemporary practice of medicine which went beyond the usual jokes about doctors. He has firm ideas about the treatment of his own condition according to the prevailing theory of the humors (1,xi) and about the superiority of gentle balms and syrups over harsh purgatives and the psychological importance of the soothing bedside manner (1, Introduction); he is scathing about the medical jargon which doctors use to blind the man in the street with science (1,iv). Marcos' poor health in Italy gives rise to a disquisition on the superior quality of the water in various parts of Spain compared with that of Italy (3, Introduction). Music, too, was a lifetime interest of Espinel, and, as with medicine, he often uses comparisons and examples from this field to illustrate his point (1,v) and displays an impressive knowledge of musical theory (3,v). Marcos, in his encounter with the *hidalgo* looking for a tutor for his children, expatiates on the third of Espinel's favorite subjects — education and, in particular, on the qualities of the perfect teacher who seems, in his eyes, to combine the wisdom of Solomon with the patience of Job.

In other cases, the digressions have a bearing upon the aims and methods pursued by Espinel in writing *Marcos de Obregón*. He displays a special interest in the function of the human memory (3,xiv) and in promoting the delights of good talk (1,xix), while condemning the evils of loquacity (1, xviii). The relevance for a book of memoirs, mostly made up of recollections from the past in conversation with a hermit, is obvious. This group of digressions leads naturally into the fourth category of "organic" or thematic digressions, moral in tone, which underline the central message of the book. For Espinel, the happy and fulfilled human being is one whose life is controlled by patience (1,xii; 2,ix), moderation (1,ix) and steadfastness (1,xvii); in applying these ideas to his personal conduct, such a man will avoid extremes, in questions of honor, for example (3,vii); he will also be acutely aware, as was Marcos, of the need to guard against the dangers of sloth (1,vi; 2,vi).

The digressions, then, contribute to the miscellany aspect of *Marcos de Obregón*, reflect Espinel's special interests, and justify and illustrate the aims of the book. By and large, they are pertinent to the theme and help to form a picture of the Squire as a man of his time, sensible in his approach to the problem of life and mindful of the hereafter. They develop naturally from Marcos' adventures, providing a moral commentary which gives depth and perspective to the novel, breaking up a succession of episodes. In taking the decision to make his moralizing explicit, Espinel is in good company; Fielding and Tolstoy, for instance, shared his opinion. He is careful to weld his digressions on to the body of the narrative, using them to introduce or add a conclusion to Marcos' adventures and to relate the particulars of those escapades to general principles. He often inserts fables, anecdotes, and examples from among his famous contemporaries to illustrate this material and lend variety. In the pursuit of this variety, however, he does not lose sight of the Neo-Aristotelian principle that the parts of a work should combine to form a harmonious whole, and he acknowledges when he departs from this precept as when, after dealing with the question of royal favorites, he writes: "Chance sometimes offers subjects which divert one from the main object, as has happened to me in this parenthesis in which I have left my story to deal with things which are not of my calling . . ." (II,104). On other occasions, he cuts short a digression or a series of illustrations "in order to avoid prolixity" (II,47). On the whole, however, the digressions are in accordance with the literary doctrine of the day and are especially appropriate to the technique of a writer like Espinel whose dedication to Horace and the precept of "prodesse et delectare" ("to give profit and delight") was well known. In his hands, the novel takes on the feel of a rambling sermon in which the preacher brings in a wide variety of examples to illustrate his text. In Espinel's case, the "text" of patience and moderation may owe something of its insistence to the feelings of guilt produced by his immoderate behavior in his years as a priest in Ronda. That, however, is only a tempting but unsubstantiated speculation.

XI   *The Novelistic Interpolations*

Although the episodes in question are examined in the critical analysis of *Marcos de Obregón* (see Chapter 4, Sections III, XI, XIII, XV, and XVI), it is helpful to look at the interpolations as a group against the background of current literary theory and practice and to see what relation, if any, exists between these apparent concessions to variety and the main themes of the work as a whole.[29] The intercalation of stories often unrelated to the main plot into a longer piece of imaginative literature dates back to Classical times and can be found in Spain from the chivalresque fiction of the Middle Ages onward. As with the digressions, justification for the technique is to be found in Neo-Aristotelian literary theory concerning the harmonious relationship of the parts of a work to the whole. The introduction of detachable stories lends variety to a string of episodes featuring the protagonist of a novel; in Part I of *Don Quixote*, Cervantes gave examples of use of this technique varying from stories which are told in the absence of the hero to adventures which could be seen as slices of the knight's life. In the period between the publication of Part I and the composition of the continuation, however, there was obviously criticism of the lack of relevance of some of this material to the body of the work because, although in the famous Chapter 44 of Part II Cervantes answers his critics and defends the relevance of his interpolations, he is careful to use the device more sparingly in Part II. Mateo Alemán, on the other hand, introduces four completely separable novelettes into *Guzmán de Alfarache*, narrated by characters who have no other function in the work.

Against this background of the theory and practice of the day in relation to interpolated material, Espinel adopts a compromise position. His stories are based on the same literary traditions available to his contemporaries (the Italian short story, chivalresque and Byzantine fiction, accounts of voyages of exploration, the picaresque genre, the Moorish novel); but he is careful to involve his Squire either as a leading figure in the affairs of Doña Mergelina de Aybar, in the scenes of captivity in Algiers and the brush with the courtesan Camila, as counselor in the dénouement of the sad tale of Aurelio, or as sympathetic listener to the young *pícaro*'s life story and the account of Dr. Sagredo's fabulous adventures in the New World. At no stage is Marcos absent from the proceedings, as happens when Don Quixote is upstairs asleep while the tale of *El curioso impertinente (The Man Who Was Too Curious for His Own Good)* is being read to the guests at an inn; nor is the narrator of the New World adventures, for example, unconnected with Marcos' life story, as is the case with the priest who relates *Ozmín y Daraja* in the *Guzmán*.

The group of episodes involving Marcos' service with Dr. Sagredo and his wife, which constitutes most of the first flashback of *Marcos de Obregón* (1,ii–vi), is loosely based upon stories from the *Decameron*. [30] Espinel's debt to Boccaccio should not, however, blind us to the masterly way he has adapted the Italianate plot of the affair between the haughty Doña Mergelina and the barber's lad to a setting of life in the old Moorish quarter of Madrid and to his dual purpose of entertaining and teaching. Like the opening chapters of the *Quixote*, Marcos' involvement with the Sagredos sets the pattern for the rest of the work, and the sequence may have been written in the "few exercise books" (I,34) referred to in the Prologue, and circulated among Espinel's friends for comment and criticism. In these early *descansos* (or chapters), we are introduced to the central character and to his style of operation in the context of an exemplary tale in which the arrogance and foolishness of the doctor's wife are sharply criticized by Marcos. The barber's boy's skill on the guitar finds the weak spot in Doña Mergelina, and she becomes foolishly fond of the boy; blind to his sores, she purrs over him as she wipes him clean of the contents of a chamber pot accidentally poured over him as he came to visit her. An intimate supper is interrupted by the unexpected arrival of her husband. Marcos twice saves the day as he lures a dog away from the intruder's hideaway and blames the noise made by the would-be lovers on the mule. Doña Mergelina does not, however, escape unscathed, receiving a beating intended for the mule and a lecture from Marcos on her folly. The incidents themselves, although owing something to the popular theater and the Italian short story, are described in a lively fashion within a framework of local color and custom which reflects, with a delicacy of touch reminiscent of the *Lazarillo de Tormes*, the austere life of the Sagredos, the doctor's irascibility, pedantry, and interest in soldiering, and the wife's pampered but empty life. Marcos' intervention is timely, his advice pertinent. When, at the end of *Marcos de Obregón*, Dr. Sagredo fortuitously meets up with Marcos and is miraculously reunited with Doña Mergelina, whom he believed dead, Espinel is using the Aristotelian technique of chance reunions (*agniciones*) to round off his interpolation and show, perhaps, that the pair have been purged of their faults as a result of heeding Marcos' advice and of their harrowing experiences. The first part of the sequence is an admirable curtain-raiser for the book, serving to introduce the protagonist and give an example of Espinel's powers as a writer; the second part shows him following current trends in tying up the loose threads of his narrative.

The adventures of Marcos in Algiers and the circumstances leading up to his capture (2, viii–xiii) indicate clearly that, whether or not Espinel ever was taken by pirates and held in captivity, the Moorish interpolation is rooted in a literary tradition, not in lived experience.[31] Echoes of Gil Polo, Cervantes, Mateo Alemán and Ginés Pérez de Hita are united with local color drawn from descriptive geographies of North Africa to form a diverting succession of scenes which again serve to underline Marcos' function as a counselor and schemer. Given the job of acting as tutor to the son and daughter of his renegade captor, Marcos, with the tacit acquiescence of the father, who still preserves his respect for the old ways, indoctrinates the two in the Catholic faith. In the case of the daughter, the use of the well-worn motif of conversion by love peters out because, if Marcos at first seems to encourage the girl's youthful passion, he later has to backtrack and plead a difference in age. Presumably it is one thing to send your *alter ego* off to Algiers; it is quite another to bring him back with a wife. Nevertheless, the sequence is entertaining and shows Marcos devising schemes to whisper his confidences to the girl under the noses of the parents and to let the King know that his favorite is robbing him by training a bird to talk. The didactic element consists of defending and promoting the true faith and stressing the patience in adversity of the protagonist whose ingenuity wins him his freedom. As in the case of the Sagredos, Espinel rounds off the story of the renegade's children by having them cross Marcos' path again by chance toward the end of the third *relación* (3,xvi) to be presented as shining examples of devotion to the Catholic faith. Perhaps the most interesting figure to emerge from the Moorish adventure, however, is the renegade himself. In him, Espinel reflects the resentment felt by the *moriscos* at being discriminated against by Spanish society and excluded from positions for which their talents would otherwise fit them. Marcos' attempts to defend the legislation concerning purity of ancestry (*limpieza de sangre*) lack conviction, and as Carrasco Urgoiti has pointed out, the sympathetic portrayal of the renegade and his hankering for the Spanish way of life make Espinel's position, like that of Cervantes, ambiguous.[32]

Two important facets of Marcos' character — his capacity for giving sound advice and his resourcefulness — are illustrated by the two interpolations in the Squire's Italian experience.[33] The tale of suspicion and revenge told by the melancholy noble, Aurelio (3,v–vii), with its gory dénouement showing the bodies of the suspected lover, the servant who knew too much, and the starving wife, is based upon the *Decameron* and *Orlando Furioso* and represents the darker side of the Italianate tradition; the Camila episode (3,viii–ix), in which Marcos outsmarts the courtesan with designs on his money, again echoes Boccaccio but this time the lighthearted side which stresses women's wiles. In both these Italian encounters, Marcos emerges with an enhanced reputation: in the first, his humane advice on love and honor turns Aurelio back from the ultimate, Calderonian tragedy of killing his wife on suspicion of adultery, without adequate proof; in the second, Camila is defeated by one of Marcos' stratagems. Espinel captures the Gothic atmosphere of the first tale with a sparing but well-observed description of the emptiness and gloom of the house, the unease of the servants, and the stark horror of that scene in the garden with the dismembered heart of the supposed lover to symbolize the tragedy. The Camila episode catches the decadent flavor of the fast-moving deceptions of a *novela cortesana* (courtly tale) of the period.

The *pícaro's* story (3,xv) is usually omitted from the list of Espinel's interpolations, and yet it constitutes a picaresque novel in miniature in which a witty rogue tells of stealing four *reales* (coins) from his father, leaving his home in Torreperogil only to lose his money gambling, have his sleep on a bench disturbed by foraging pigs, and enter the service of a young friar on his way to study in Alcalá. On the recommendation of his master, he is accepted as a novice in a monastery of the order but thrown out when discovered stealing from the kitchen. He evades his pursuers by leading them into a swarm of bees. It is at this stage of his life that the *pícaro* meets Marcos, and there is an interesting contrast in attitude at the end of their encounter when both stress the need to look out for one's own interests in this life but Marcos adds that this should be done without harming a third party.

Models for the adventures of Dr. Sagredo and his wife on the expedition to the Straits of Magellan (3,xix–xxiii) are not difficult to find in the Byzantine and chivalresque novels, the accounts of voyages of discovery, the continuations of the *Lazarillo* and even in the *Odyssey*.[34] The tale told by Dr. Sagredo as Marcos and he are held prisoner by bandits is a curious mixture of fact and fantasy: the storms at sea, the attempts to colonize and proselytize, the description of flora and fauna have an eye-witness quality, reflecting the work of the New World historians; the giants and monsters, though traces of them may be found in travelers' tales, properly belong to the novels of high adventure popular in Espinel's day. As with the rogue's story, Marcos' function in relation to Dr. Sagredo's fantastic yarn is simply that of interested listener. Whereas, however, at the end of the rascal's account, Marcos makes clear the difference between his attitude and the selfishness of the lad, the Squire does little more when the doctor has finished than offer advice on the sharing of grief for the "lost" Doña Mergelina. Nevertheless, this does not mean that Dr. Sagredo's fantastic adventures have nothing to tell us in respect of the themes of *Marcos de Obregón*. It is curious to note, for example, how as if in a dream sequence the good doctor abandons the pedantry, choler, and lack of dedication for which he was criticized in his first appearance in the book and becomes a stouthearted, resourceful replica of Marcos himself in the adventures. He never despairs; he always comes up with a scheme to get his fellow-mariners out of trouble. The adventures in the New World are just as much a piece of wish-fulfillment for Dr. Sagredo as are the exploits of Marcos for Espinel himself.

There is, then, a oneness about the interpolations, in spite of their range of source, mood, and venue. They underline the message of common sense, courage, and resilience which is central to the book as a whole, while at the same time, fulfilling a need for variety and entertainment through which *Marcos de Obregón* reflects a range of literary theories current in early seventeenth century Spain.

XII   *Some Stylistic Features*

Zamora Vicente, as the title of his essay on *Marcos de Obregón* suggests, pays particular attention to the combination of tradition and originality in the work of Espinel. He makes the point that, although his style is "closer to Herrera than to Góngora,"[35] Espinel's approach to certain areas, particularly the description of Nature, is strikingly original. Many times in the course of the novel, Espinel emphasizes his desire to describe things "with the simplicity and clarity with which they happened" (II,15); the language should be so "easy and clear as not to give the reader trouble understanding it" (II,308). By the same token, the author pours scorn on obscurity and excess, ridiculing the use of medical jargon as "so much pedantry" (I,79) and gently satirizing the Count of Lemos' doctor for his reluctance to call a spade a spade and the wife of Mami Reys for her pompous speech during her escape from Algiers about "horrible marine monsters in the profound abysses of the profound (sic) caverns of the sea" (II,112). Clearly, it is not just doctors and hysterical females that the writer has in mind but pretentiousness in language wherever it is to be found, and the less talented followers of Góngora would doubtless not miss the point.

The mention of Herrera in connection with Espinel's prose style recalls our earlier remarks on certain features of his poetry (see Chapter II, Section IX). Both writers share a feeling for color, especially in Nature. Espinel is particularly sensitive to the hues of dawn: the rays of the morning sun "midway between green and greenish-yellow, a sign of rain" (I,213); or "the sun large and yellowish in color" (I,134) with a flock of sheep bumping against each other as they look to the sky for the approach of a storm. His descriptions of storms on land and sea are unusually vivid for a Golden Age writer. The storm which traps Marcos in the sanctuary with the hermit, for example, is brought to life by a series of exclamations: "Heavens, and what continuous and miserable thunder! What enormous hailstones! What great persistence!" (I,139); the one which causes the Squire to take shelter on the way to Milan is enlivened by touches such as: "We could not see a light except through the eyes of the horse which guided us" (II,125–6). In both cases, Espinel achieves greater effect by relating the storms to his own experience of rough weather in the mountains of Ronda. Storms at sea, too, are an exciting aspect of *Marcos de Obregón*. In one such storm, Espinel describes the stern of the ship groaning "like a person lamenting" (II,51), the sailors being sick and the boatswain, in an attempt to rescue his parrot, caught "like Absalom" (II,53) by his beard in the rigging.

The same eye for arresting detail oversees Espinel's descriptions of Nature in quieter moods. A "superhuman fragrance" (II,57) of honeysuckle, for instance, pervades the delightful spot Marcos finds on the island of Cabrera; the smell of oranges and lemons is associated with Málaga and some of the villages of Espinel's beloved Andalusia. "Beloved" that is, except perhaps for his home town of Ronda, the descriptions of which illustrate the writer's ambivalent attitude. On the one hand, Ronda symbolizes all that is home — a place to return to thankfully, to remember nostalgically; on the other, Ronda's remoteness and small-town attitudes tend to drive its sons away. Akin to Herrera's symbolic landscapes, we have the violence of storms and the peace of a natural beauty spot to represent the extremes of Espinel's temperament, together with a love-hate attitude toward Ronda which is also reflected in his poems. One of the curiosities of the Málaga area is seized upon by Espinel for its symbolism. Near Casarabonela there are, we are told, two jets of water issuing in opposite directions from a rock. On one side, the water is warm, the vegetation flourishing; on the other, the water is cold and there are few leaves on the plants. The result is that: "Everything that looks towards Málaga is very spring-like and all that faces Ronda, very wintry; and all the way is like that" (I,243). We are reminded of the warm stream of fulfillment and the cold stream of failure in "The House of Memory." The message emanating from the description seems to be "Go hence, young man." And that, of course, is what Espinel did to escape from the hostility he found on his return to Ronda.

As the account of the natural descriptions in *Marcos de Obregón* indicates, there are parallels between the range and tenor of the descriptive passages in *Miscellaneous Verse* and *Marcos de Obregón*. Personal portraits varying from the flattering to the satirical can be found in both works. Espinel's stylized poetic tribute to a patron's future wife in *Miscellaneous Verse* (133–35) is matched by the statuesque beauty of Aurelio's wife in *Marcos de Obregón* (II,178); his cruel self-portrait in verse (161) has the same astringent quality as his descriptions in prose of the ugly wife of an innkeeper (I, 180–81) and of the posturing of the Portuguese and the Venetian (II, 183–85). Equally, in both works, flattery of actual or potential patrons leads to the "set piece" description in which Espinel displays his wares as a writer or portrays an aristocrat in a deferential light. In this category are some of the poems dedicated to men of position and influence in the collection of verse and the anecdotes told about, for example, the Marquis of las Navas (II,11–15) or the description of the St. John's Day tournament (II,90–95) in the novel. As in *Miscellaneous Verse*, Espinel can occasionally explore the horrors of graveyards, as in the tale of the San Ginés tomb (I,93–98), or present an awesome spectacle with the dead and dying figures which represent Aurelio's revenge (II,172–73). He matches the impressive description of the domain of Memory in "The House of Memory" with the giants and sea monsters, storms and shipwrecks of Dr. Sagredo's adventures in the New World.

Another feature of the style of *Marcos de Obregón* which has links with Espinel's poetry are the references to music and the use of music as a basis of comparisons. When Marcos wishes to point to the absurdity of an old man marrying a young girl, it is to music that he turns for his simile: ". . . it is like wanting a *basso profundo* and a soprano to sing the same part" (I,93). Music is shown as having a capacity to lead human thoughts toward contemplation of the Creator (II,224) and to cause people to imitate its mood (II,159). It is in such ways that Espinel's interest in and knowledge of music shines through the pages of *Marcos de Obregón*.

In prose and poetry, Espinel shows a fondness for antithesis. The opposition of fire and ice, peace and war, etc., in his lyrics is mirrored in the opening of the novel when the author describes how he was torn by extremes before deciding to publish *Marcos de Obregón*: ". . . confidence and timorousness fought a fierce internal battle within me" (I,31). This use of antithetical expressions, which is a constant of Espinel's style in prose and verse, may, like his fondness for extremes in Nature, be related to the polarities of his choleric temperament. In his life, as in his writings, he tended to oscillate between violence and calm. Although the hidden message of the novel is the search for *paciencia* — stoical acceptance of the blows of life — a tension is produced in the work by the feeling that the Squire, like his creator, has not received his just deserts, and, occasionally, this produces an outburst of anger or a feeling of resentment. This is what happens in the poem addressed to the Bishop of Málaga; it occurs, too, when Marcos inveighs against backbiting (I, 122–123) or speaks of his life of trouble and misfortune. Marcos feels himself a victim of hostile Fortune, just as does Espinel's Petrarchan mask, Liseo. They both long for the Horatian peace of the countryside, as evinced by Marcos' admiration for the way of life of Pedro Jiménez Espinel (3,xvii) and the "Beatus ille" pronounced by Liseo in the eclogue, "Ay, apacible y sosegada vida" ("Oh peaceful and calm life"; 137–46): in both, as in Espinel himself, there is a tension which only Tolstoy's "Patience and time, time and patience" will cure.

These, then, are some aspects of the style of *Marcos de Obregón* which can be related also to *Miscellaneous Verse*. Much admired in his day as an elegant versifier, Espinel has been praised by later generations of critics for his prose style. In addition to its flowing rhythm and directness, it is a way of writing which displays special aptitude for description and a fondness for musical analogies. Espinel's style is also given a tension and vitality, however, which prevents it from becoming honeyed, by the antitheses and abundant vocabulary associated with hostile Fortune, which may stem from the character of the author and from his response to the changing times of the reign of Philip III.

CHAPTER 4

Marcos de Obregón: *Critical Analysis*

I *Date of Composition*

IN view of the relative complication of the time-sequence presented in *Marcos de Obregón* and of the tie-up between the events of the Squire's life and those of his creator, it would be wise at the outset to establish, as closely as possible, the date of composition.[1] The preliminaries to the novel, in which Espinel is shown to have received the necessary official approval and permission to publish, belong to the year 1617, although the novel did not actually appear until the following year. In the Prologue, however, Espinel tells us that his diffidence concerning the work was partially overcome by the encouragement of distinguished literary friends among whom he circulated the manuscript. He also goes on to relate how "a certain gentleman" passed off as his own one of the early episodes which he had read in the circulated draft.

Internal evidence points to a period of composition of about three years, from 1614 to 1616, during which time, as Espinel modestly states, he was: "doubtful whether he would launch this poor SQUIRE, empty of virtues and full of troubles . . ." (I,31). Reference to recent events, such as the death of Francisco de Silva and the fall of Mámora and to figures with whom Espinel associated help to pinpoint this period. The anecdote of the two students who come across the grave of the lovers of Antequera, which is recounted in the Prologue as an encouragement to the reader to look for the hidden meaning beneath the surface of the narrative, also suggests the probable date of composition by its use of the Latin tag *Conditur unio*, with its double meaning of "A union is buried" and "A treasure is hidden." The same Latin phrase was used by Espinel in a poem which he entered for a competition in Toledo in 1616.

104

II *Prefatory Material*

The two prologues which follow the dedication to the celebrated Maecenas, Don Bernardo de Sandoval y Rojas, Cardinal Archbishop of Toledo, are of interest because, in addition to the usual mock-humility of an author presenting his work to a patron and to the reading public, Espinel adopts attitudes which give us an important clue to the proper understanding of the rest of the book.[2] Following the principles outlined by his "master" Horace, Espinel wants his work to be so designed and proportioned as to please and instruct his readers in order that: "morality has room for delight and delight space for teaching" (I,33). He follows the lead of some authors of picaresque novels (*Lazarillo* and *Guzmán de Alfarache* are examples) who, possibly nervous of officialdom, urge their readers to look beneath the surface of the lighthearted narrative for a hidden meaning. In Espinel's case, the reason could hardly be that he had similar fears of official reaction to his innocuous tale. Only one short passage ever attracted the attention of the Inquisition. And yet the author makes the assertion of the existence of a hidden meaning more than a routine formula by illustrating it with a typical cautionary tale concerning the two students, the alert one of whom, seeing the double meaning of the Latin phrase *Conditur unio*, finds a valuable pearl in the tomb of the lovers of Antequera. Espinel's insistence is curious: "I would not like anyone, in what I write, to be satisfied with reading the surface, because there is not a single page in my SQUIRE which does not bear a particular intention beyond that which is apparent" (I,38).[3]

In addition to the Horatian double aim and the claim to a second, hidden layer of meaning, the two prologues also reveal the link between Espinel and Marcos which is part of the special attraction of the work. In the first prologue, Espinel, as the real author, is seen as having his determination to publish the book undermined by attacks of gout; in the second, Marcos, the protagonist-narrator, emerges as a gout-ridden old pensioner living out the last years of his life in quarters not dissimilar to those occupied by the ailing Espinel. Like his creator, Marcos addresses the Archbishop of Toledo as his patron; he shares with Espinel the twin aims of delight and instruction and the desire to write in a pleasing style, suited to general taste. Thus, even in the prefatory material, Espinel begins to create the illusion that his Squire is an *alter ego*, with the same aspirations, attitudes, and tastes as his creator; at the same time, he allows the reader increasingly to feel that he is following the steps of a character who has achieved a degree of autonomy unusual in the seventeenth-century novel.

It may be too that, instead of looking between the lines of the work for Espinel's friends masquerading as characters or for some other clue to the secret hidden, like the pearl, in every page, we would do well to consider a simpler "secret" referred to in the second prologue. Marcos, dedicating "this long account of my life" (I,39) to the Archbishop, states that it also contains a secret related to his desire to show, amid misfortunes and adversity, how important it is for poor squires like himself to face up bravely to the perils of time and fortune, cling to life, and continue to appreciate the handiwork of the Creator of the universe. This, then, may well be the "secret" message of Espinel-Marcos, announced in both prologues and illustrated in the ensuing chapters, a message which distinguishes *Marcos de Obregón* from the picaresque novels with which it is so often misleadingly compared: a smiling acceptance of adversity which eschews excess and opts for moderation in all things. The aged Marcos and his creator have learned, through their experience of a life which has never reached the heights, philosophical gifts of patience, tolerance, and moderation which are a fundamental part of the tone and attitude of the book and of the stance adopted by an aged Espinel and an aged Marcos before the buffetings of a real and fictionalized life.

Thus does Espinel step into the shoes of his creation, the charity pensioner with a local reputation as a quack doctor, prescribing soothing remedies, whispering soothing prayers, dressing to impress the gullible, and like a doctor in a Molière or Beaumarchais play, losing only half his patients — the half that tells no tales.

III   *The Point of View*

The opening chapters of *Marcos de Obregón*, in which the Squire reminisces about his service with the choleric Dr. Sagredo and his flighty wife, Doña Mergelina de Aybar, and about his meeting with the *hidalgo* seeking a tutor for his sons, are typical of Espinel's method and approach. In them, the protagonist Marcos relates, in a leisurely fashion, diverting episodes concerning Doña Mergelina's

abortive affair with the barber's lad or the *hidalgo*'s encounter with a
herd of cows interwoven with moral homilies giving an old man's
views on the virtue of patience, the dangers of idleness, the delights
of music, the education of the young, and the mumbo-jumbo associated with the practice of medicine. The episodes are lively,
echoing Boccaccio's treatment of the deception of husbands, and
recalling the pace and atmosphere of a picaresque novel.[4] The sexual frankness of the Italian source, however, has been replaced by a
fastidious elegance of expression, and the picaresque touches are
not allied to that slanted vision of the world which gives the true
picaresque its impact. Although there is a flavor here and there of
the *Lazarillo*, the *Buscón* (*The Sharper*) and *Guzmán de
Alfarache* — in the comic description of the barber's boy using his
guitar-playing as an excuse to scratch his infected wrists, the "attack" on the gentleman by the herd of cows, and in the types described in the later scene — the part played by Marcos in these
incidents differs from that of the self-preserving *pícaro*. There is a
tutor's sanctimoniousness about the Squire as he tries to save Doña
Mergelina from adultery or the gentleman from the cows which
betokens a philosophy of life based upon class values entirely distinct from those of Lázaro, Pablos, or Guzmán.

The special charm of these early chapters, however, lies not in the
unremarkable combination of episode and moral commentary but in
establishing the angle of vision of the author and his creation, the
aged Squire writing his memoirs in the tranquil atmosphere of the
pensioners' home of Santa Catalina de los Donados. The use of the
term "angle of vision" here is intended to cover several aspects of
the same process: the further identification which we saw emerging
in the prologues between Espinel and Marcos; the time-sequence
imposed upon the novel; the tone and attitudes which color the
narrative.[5]

The feeling of identification between the author and the Squire is
reinforced by references to age, gout, and places from, as it were, a
common past. Both are in the last years of their lives; they are both
afflicted with gout, and the description of the symptoms and treatment of it, in line with the theory of humors, has the ring of truth. It
is as natural that Marcos should fear the cold of Old Castile as that
Espinel — and, later in the novel, Marcos too — should find the
climate of northern Italy bad for his health. Marcos' recollection of
his period of service with the Sagredos is triggered by a disquisition

on patience, a virtue which Dr. Sagredo singularly lacked. Espinel himself was a choleric type, certainly up to his move to Madrid, and only later in life did he manage to live down his reputation for asperity. At the same time, the Sagredo phase is marked by a love of music and an excellence in performance which is also common to both creator and creature. It is as though Espinel is grafting on to his protagonist's present and past life qualities associated with his own. Although Espinel makes a conventional, Hitchcock-like appearance as the friend of Marcos, associated with the Capilla del Obispo, who recommends him to the Sagredos, the chain of references linking Marcos and Espinel is too continuous to allow this nod in the direction of convention to distract us. Doña Mergelina, for instance, frequents that same Church of San Andrés which Espinel served for twenty-five years; footpads lurk in the alley beside the church, as they did in Espinel's time; and a name linked with the church and with Espinel in documents of the day, that of Juan de Vergara, is used, probably as a private joke, for the master of Doña Mergelina's young man and as an expert in hair-dyeing known to the lady.[6] Marcos' obvious familiarity with Espinel's birthplace of Ronda is further evidence of this common vision, reinforced in later chapters.

This community of viewpoint is also apparent in the presentation of the time-sequence in the novel. The work opens "a few days ago" (I,43) as the aged Marcos, in his capacity as quack doctor curing by spells, is treating a patient. Abuse of his efforts by a passer-by provokes a lecture on patience, illustrated by examples of men of breeding and good taste whom Espinel admired. This lecture, in its turn, leads into a flashback to the Sagredo episode, designed to show the dangers of shortness of temper (1,ii–vi). In a later meeting with Dr. Sagredo (II,263), the mention of Diego Flores de Valdés' departure for the New World puts the date of Marcos' then-terminated service with the doctor and his wife at about 1581, although on the basis of Marcos' own timing, it would be after his return from Italy in 1584. Espinel's intention, however, is clear: to make Marcos recall a period in his life some thirty years before the opening of the story, which we have earlier set at between 1614 and 1616. And yet there is evidence of confusion and split-level thinking concerning the protagonist's age. When he first meets Doña Mergelina, he regards her with interest and approval "although an old man incapable of such appetites" (I,50); when Doña Mergelina offers him marriage with a young relative, his reactions show that he thinks of himself as old and white-haired — older than he would have been in the early 1580's. He pours scorn on marriages between men of fifty and young girls of fifteen or sixteen. These lapses may be evidence of carelessness of composition. We should not allow them, however, to obscure our appreciation of the overall framework, the grand design of the interlocked time-cycles: the first coincides with Espinel-Marcos' decision to write his memoirs from the vantage point of old age; the second covers the period from childhood to old age in flashback form and not in chronological sequence. Another way to look at the "lapses" is to see them as the superimposition of one time-scale upon another. They serve to remind us that, within the flashbacks, we are dealing with time remembered, time passed through the filter of memory as Marcos and his creator look back at a joint life, embroidered and enlivened by fictional episodes, in which the lessons of age and experience are used to invest events with a significance which they were not seen to have when they occurred. Thus, Marcos thinks like an old man when re-living the episodes of his youth.

To some extent, this backward-looking process governs the tone and attitude of the work. Sermons on the inner beauty of the soul, on the virtues of preserving a discreet silence, and of learning by our mistakes form part of the "good and salutary advice" (I, 76) offered to Doña Mergelina by her moral counselor. The *hidalgo*, in his turn, is treated to a discourse on the philosophy of education and the qualities of an ideal tutor. In both cases, the worthy advice is in marked contrast to the undignified episodes in which the two become involved. Doña Mergelina, in a series of scenes reminiscent of a Feydeau farce, tries to deceive her husband and gets a beating intended for the mule; the gentleman takes his stand on the Puente de Segovia against a herd of cows and is discomfited. The contrast is made more effective by the feeling that the story improves in the remembrance, receiving a gloss which stems from the accumulated wisdom of Marcos-Espinel's experience of life and which gives it a distinctive and non-picaresque flavor. The moralizing, which some critics have found tedious, is perhaps lightened by the interplay of time-levels which gives an added dimension to the work. Equally, it produces a curious dichotomy: on the one hand, Marcos projects himself back into the picaresque spirit of the barber's boy episode and describes him as suffering from a form of scabies or as arriving on one occasion covered in the contents of somebody's chamber pot;

on the other hand, he draws back from using the vernacular to describe the location of the Count of Lemos' hemorroids. The existence of these levels, affecting the presentation of the protagonist, the time-sequence, and the tone of the work, although not always perfectly conceived or executed, makes *Marcos de Obregón*, on the evidence of these early chapters, an attempt at novelized memoirs which employs techniques exploited in the subsequent history of modern European literature in the areas of the autonomous character (Unamuno, Pirandello) and the interaction of time and memory (Proust).

IV   *Flashback*

Stealing away from his lodgings early one morning, Marcos goes to pray at a little chapel (*humilladero*) attached to the Ermita (Hermitage) del Santo Angel de la Guarda on the far side of the Puente de Segovia. The hermit engages him in conversation and invites him to shelter from the storm which has just broken. In this way the author, in *Descanso* viii, leads us into the second flashback in which, in talking to the hermit, Marcos reviews his early life from his childhood in Ronda in the 1550's up to his service with the Sagredos in the 1580's. These reminiscences take us from the dawn of one day until the waters go down two days later, that is in terms of the time taken to narrate them; as a function of Marcos' memory, they occupy some thirty years. We admire the stamina of the hermit as, for the best part of three days, he listens to the story of Marcos' schooldays in Ronda, his period as a student in Salamanca, his travels and adventures in various parts of Spain, his captivity in Algiers, his visit to Italy, and finally, his service with the Sagredos.

At this point in the narrative, the middle of the third and final part or *relación*, Marcos should logically take his leave of the hermit since we have reached a point in his life immediately preceding his taking shelter in the roadside chapel. Through an oversight, however, pointed out by Gili Gaya,[7] Espinel allows Marcos to continue his story with further travels in Andalusia and a second meeting with Dr. Sagredo who, in his turn, recounts his fantastic adventures on the high seas on a trip to the Straits of Magellan, as a result of which his wife was lost, presumed drowned. It is only after she has been providentially restored to him and when the reunited group has gone back to Madrid that Espinel allows his protagonist to say goodbye to the hermit (3,xxv). This is clearly twelve chapters too late. A confusion seems to have arisen in Espinel's mind between the two separate meetings with the Sagredos. However that may be, the true moment for Marcos to say goodbye to the hermit is at the end of 3,xiii: "I wandered about Madrid for a few days, where I became tutor and squire to Dr. Sagredo and his wife Doña Mergelina de Aybar until I left them or they left me" (II,221).

Some editions, for instance those of 1804 (Mateo Repullés), 1868 (Juan Cuesta), and the two published by Pérez de Guzmán in 1881 and 1883, rectify the error by bringing the leavetaking paragraph of the penultimate chapter of the book back to the end of *Descanso* xiii of the final *relación*. E. Muret[8] offers the hypothesis of a page becoming misplaced in the printing of the first edition and the error being continued thereafter, but a more likely explanation is that, as with mistakes and contradictions concerning Marcos' age, we are dealing with a *lapsus* by Espinel arising out of the fictionalization of lived experience. In a curious way, this evidence of the fallibility of the human memory adds conviction to a novel which deals with time remembered and strengthens the bond between Espinel and his creation.

The intricacies of the chronological structure of the novel should not, however, blind us to its other qualities. In the transitional chapter in the chapel or *humilladero* (1,viii), there are, for example, two good paragraphs of description, an aspect of Espinel's writing which has attracted little critical attention. He effectively describes the dawn on that stormy day, with a yellowish sun, and the sheep by the bridge bumping into each other as they look up at the threatening sky. When the storm comes, Espinel, in a few lines, conjures up a vision of thunder and lightning, the water rising quickly to cover the arches of the bridge, and the doors of the little chapel shaken by the wind.

Another feature of the chapter, which links with the angle of vision adopted by the novelist, as outlined in the previous section, is the appearance of a group of Espinel's contemporaries in a remembered episode of Marcos' earlier life. This is a different case from the citing of Don Gabriel Zapata and Don Fernando de Toledo as examples of forbearance (1,i) or of the Count of Lemos for cutting through medical jargon (1,iv), when the use of the names is a form of flattery which, at the same time, lends authority to the arguments being put forward. In using the Oviedo brothers and a fellow-priest, Alonso

Franco, as part of the action, Espinel is welding the present on to the past and making Marcos increasingly his *alter ego*. For those Oviedo brothers, "two gentlemen in religious garb, of outstanding intellect allied to prudence and goodness" (I,135), who, having invited Marcos to join them in their coach, score debating points on the subject of honor and vengeance against some thoughtless young buck who frightened the horses, are the same Bernardo and Luis de Oviedo, gentlemen of the household of the Cardinal Archbishop of Toledo, who are mentioned in the Dedication. They are joined in discussion by Maestro Alonso Franco, friend of Espinel, priest at San Andrés and named as executor in the novelist's will. Thus does the present of Espinel, the time when he was writing the book and looking for a patron, merge with the remembered past of Marcos; thus do Espinel's acquaintances cross the boundary from fact into fiction and come to people Marcos' world. It is noticeable too that they are used, as were Gabriel de Zapata and Fernando de Toledo in a more straightforward fashion, to underline that message of *paciencia* which seems to link Espinel's turbulent past to his tranquil present and constitute an underlying theme of the work.

V   *Ronda*

The recurring motifs which serve to remind us that Marcos and Espinel are one and the same are a common birthplace, a common affliction, and a reputation as a poet and musician. There are chains of references to these in the pages of *Marcos de Obregón*. Echoing the opening of the account by Quevedo's Pablos of his adventures, Marcos begins his story to the hermit with the words: "I, sir, . . . am from Ronda, a city set upon very high crags and sheer ravines, greatly beset, as a general rule, by fierce west and east winds . . ." (I,140). Espinel and Marcos share a love-hate relationship with this remote Andalusian hill-town. In his *Miscellaneous Verse*, Espinel waxes sentimental about his return to his "dear homeland" (69) after his travels through Spain, and his Italian period produced poems full of nostalgia for his native town. The mood changes, however, once Espinel has settled again in Ronda and felt his ambition stifled by its remoteness, its provincial outlook, and its atmosphere of envy and spite. In the poem addressed to Dr. Luis de Castilla, Espinel explains: "In other places I am a Midas, an Apollo,/ Here I am poor and ill-regarded . . ." (120). By the time Espinel came to write

Marcos de Obregón, he was settled in Madrid in a good position which allowed him to pursue his twin interests in music and literature, and so his attitude had mellowed. There are nostalgic references in *Marcos* to people, places, and traditions associated with his home town. Nevertheless, Marcos, like his creator, makes it clear on occasion that if he were to make his mark, it would be necessary to leave the remoteness of Ronda because: "if I don't do any more than my neighbors, I shall remain as ignorant as they are" (I,144).

The beginning of Marcos' reminiscences in the roadside chapel also serves to remind us of the account of the lives of service given in picaresque novels and to note the differences in the case of Marcos. One of the distinguishing features to emerge early in such accounts is the genealogy of the protagonist. The *pícaro*'s heredity combines with his environment and upbringing to corrupt him. Lázaro's father was condemned to the galleys for theft, and his widow became the common-law wife of a negro; Pablos' father, also a thief, was hung, drawn, and quartered, and his mother, a New Christian, was stigmatized as a witch and procuress; Guzmán's father was a usurer and a converted Jew, and his mother, following her family's tradition, was a prostitute. As the genre develops, the *pícaros* feel a sense of shame and inferiority because of their background and try to escape from it into the world of upright, honorable *hombres de bien* (men of good family).

Marcos, by contrast, is from a background of petty nobility and always mindful of his heritage. Like Espinel, he was descended from a family originally from the mountains near Santander which was rewarded with land in Ronda for its part in the Reconquest. Although Marcos' father seems to have come down in the world, there is no suggestion of irony when he gives his son a sword from Bilbao and tells him to go out into the world and, with God's guidance, become a respected citizen. Lázaro's mother, when she sees her son enter the service of the blind man, uses similar words but with a richness of irony which lingers in the memory as the novel progresses. Like the *pícaros*, Marcos suffers poverty because of an unfortunate start in life, but his is a genteel poverty which does not corrupt his virtuous attitude or the wholesomeness of the advice he so readily offers. He feels tenderness for his brothers and sisters and would like to help them; when, later in the novel, Marcos is battered and bruised as a result of fighting for his life in the millstream, he ruefully remembers the precepts his father taught him.

VI *Salamanca*

This difference of attitude between Marcos and the protagonists of the picaresque novels is also apparent in the adventures which befall him on the way to Salamanca and during his days as a student there. He is an advocate of moderation and forbearance, of humility and courtesy, and an enemy of idleness. Speeches on these topics interlace the episodes and denote an overt desire to offer salutary advice to the reader which, among the major picaresque novels, only the *Guzmán* shares. Marcos is careful to dissociate himself from the cruelty of picaresque hoaxes: "I do not take pride in having done this dirty trick for, after all, it was an act of revenge, a thing unworthy of a valiant breast" (I,150). His attitude toward pranks and the difficulties of student life is somewhat condescending, and as he sets out from Ronda, he invokes God's help in a simple and direct way, foreign to the tongue-in-cheek attitude of Lázaro and Pablos. His sanctimoniousness, on occasion, has more in common with Guzmán than the other leading representatives of the genre.

It cannot be denied, however, that Marcos' training in self-preservation on the way to Salamanca and at the University has a certain picaresque flavor. The way that the scoundrel at the Mesón del Potro uses flattery with the gullible Marcos to wine and dine at his expense is reminiscent of the Venta de Viveros episode in the *Buscón (The Sharper)*, and the incident was copied in Lesage's *Gil Blas de Santillane;* Marcos' revenge, having the trickster charged with stealing a planted cape, is typical of the way the rascal or *pícaro* learns how to be "bellaco con los bellacos" ("a rogue with the best of them"), as did Lazarillo. The humor is there and the richness of incident, but the episodes seem to lack conviction because Marcos' attitude is so self-righteous.

A good example of the way in which Espinel uses picaresque material without the raison d'être of the picaresque novel is offered by his occasional explorations of the humorous possibilities of the physically repugnant. When Marcos becomes separated from the rest of the group going to Salamanca, he goes to sleep under a tree and is awakened by what he takes to be ants crawling on his face. They turn out to be maggots dropping from the rotting corpse of a man over whom a woman nearby is weeping and grieving. In Salamanca, Marcos contracts scabies and, finding that the doctor's treatment of denying him water does not work, drinks his bath

water, suffers a violent attack of flatulence, vomits back into the
bath, and feels better. The starving students who put a "log" onto
the fire to cook the food Marcos brings into the lodgings find that
they are trying to burn the decomposing leg bone of a mule, and
their nausea puts one in mind of Sancho's reaction after taking the
magic balsam which was supposed to cure the ills of knights-errant.

Tastes in humor have changed over the ages, and clearly these
excursions into the repellent do not amuse us today. There is a good
deal of evidence, however, that scatological humor was appreciated
in the seventeenth century. Golden Age plays frequently feature
such incidents as part of the comic subplot, and in a serious treatise
on literary theory, the *Philosophia antigua poetica (Ancient Poetic
Philosophy)* of 1596, Alonso López Pinciano discusses different
types of humor and quotes the example of an actor breaking wind on
stage and being showered with jewels by a delighted audience.[9] In
the picaresque novel, however, such episodes are not gratuitous
explorations of the possibilities of scatological humor; they are part
of what one critic has called the "excremental vision" of the picaresque novel. They symbolize the futility of the *pícaro*'s attempts to
rise in the world. When Guzmán rides through the mire on the back
of a wild pig or gets his hands and mouth covered in excrement
when he tries to pick up a stone to throw at a dog, or when Pablos
falls into a privy and has to go home covered in filth — all these
episodes are intended to represent the *pícaro*'s failure to come to
terms with a hostile world. No such symbolism can be applied to
Marcos being covered in maggots; and when he drinks his bath
water the result is a triumph over Dr. Medina.

Another feature of the chapters devoted to Marcos' student days
is the extent to which they match up with what we know of Espinel's
university life. The records show, as we saw in Chapter 1, that
Espinel was at the University of Salamanca from 1570 to 1572; there
is no proof that he spent a further two years at the Colegio de San
Pelayo. The period supposedly spent by Marcos in Salamanca tallies
with this, and Espinel again uses the names of real people associated
with the city and the university to make his hero's story more be-
lievable and to underscore the parallelism between his own career
and that of his creation. Thus Marcos tells of contact with Father
Mancio, Francisco de Salinas, Bernardo Clavijo, Dr. Medina, Don
Enrique de Bolaños, Juan Llanos de Valdés, and Vigil de
Quiñones — all of them figures to add luster to Marcos' account of

his university days. They also help to add to the conviction that this
choleric type who gave music lessons to make a little extra money
and was unable to take up his place at San Pelayo because of a need
to go home and assume a family chaplaincy was the same as the
writer Espinel who also appears as a shadowy "Mr. So-and-So . . .
great Latinist, poet and musician" (I,145) and as "Mr. X" (I,146) in
conversation with the hermit.

VII   *Travels in Spain*

The rest of the first *relación* (or major division) is taken up with
Marcos' travels and adventures in Spain from the disruption of the
university session in April, 1572, after the imprisonment of Fray
Luis de León, until the protagonist enters the service of the Count
of Lemos some time after the end of 1574. The first stage of his
itinerary involves Marcos in a return to Málaga and Ronda on some
unspecified business to do with his studies and his family, possibly
the chaplaincy referred to at the end of the previous section. On his
return to Salamanca, Marcos seemingly decides to abandon his
studies in order to join the ill-fated fleet of Pedro Meléndez de
Avilés, struck by disease before it ever left port. Frustrated in his
ambition to go to sea, Marcos travels through northern Spain until
his restlessness is assuaged and he finds stability in the household of
the Count of Lemos in Valladolid. The failure to specify the nature
of the business which calls him home from Salamanca, combined
with the abortive mission to Santander, lend an air of aimlessness
to Marcos' wanderings, corresponding, perhaps, to that period of
Espinel's life about which we know nothing from contemporary
records but whose youthful excesses he regrets in the poetic confession addressed to his patron of the 1580's, Bishop Pacheco, and
included in *Miscellaneous Verse*. Espinel, with a prudishness which
characterizes the self-portrait he paints in *Marcos de Obregón*, sub-
stitutes anodyne adventures for these real-life escapades, adventures concerning rogues and vagabonds over whom, Walter Mitty-
like, his *alter ego* triumphs as the "real" Espinel, like a face at the
window, peeps in from time to time to add another dimension to the
relationship with the reader.

In earlier passages of the novel, one has not been inclined to make
too much of such interventions, pointing to the conventionality of
the phrase "the author of this book" as a substitute for "I".[10] In the

latter part of the first *relación*, however, particularly as Marcos comes back to Ronda, there are repeated violations of the device whereby Marcos is supposed to be telling part of the story of his life to the hermit in the chapel, violations which, while seeming to set up a more conventional relationship between Espinel as author and his reader, should rather be regarded as intensifying the illusion that Marcos is an autonomous character, able to stand away from his creator and tell of his doings. Thus, on the road to Adamuz, Marcos relates a story about a Moorish goatherd who found a way to cut off the water supply to either one of two villages in the Ronda mountains and, in attempting to play one off against the other for gain, was killed by the local inhabitants. The tale, which was told to the "author" by a real-life friend of Espinel, Juan de Luzón, is not recounted to the hermit directly but rather as a tale-within-a tale by Marcos to his traveling companions, the merchants. Marcos then goes on to tell of another incident which happened to the "author of this book" around the time of the student riots in Salamanca in 1572 when he fell into the hands of some robbers. In order to relate the dénouement, in which the author is able to have the death sentence of one of the robbers commuted to service in the galleys, the narrator has to move forward in time over twenty years. This shatters the chronology both of the journey with the merchants (1572) and of the conversation with the hermit (*ca.* 1584) and leaves us with a Marcos who has acquired the hindsight and omniscience of the true author and refers to his creator as "he": "Finally, to cut a long story short, having wandered through Spain and beyond for more than twenty years, he was reduced to the state God had marked out for him; he went to his home, which is Ronda; he became a priest, occupying a chaplaincy granted to him by Philip II . . ." (I,199–200). The ambivalence of the "I" of the narrative is further underlined when, in spite of having reminded the reader of the hermit's presence, Marcos embarks on the story of a drowning which took place "in my presence" (I,209) and that of the Marquis Luis de Haro and his son "a few years later" (I,209) than the story of his journey back home to Ronda. The aristocrats, we are told, "are still alive when this is being written and younger than the author" (I,212). Marcos thus again breaks through the conventional framework and seems to acquire the ability to move through time and look over the author's shoulder as he writes, before returning "to the present state" (I,212) and the problem of his lost mule. This sleight-of-hand effect is further emphasized by references to known aspects of Espinel's biography and personality. Although some are straightforward, as when Espinel-Marcos says he was "not very young . . . [but] very choleric and illness made me walk clumsily" (I,253), others break the time-sequence and the Marcos-Espinel identification. When Marcos, for example, goes to Málaga Cathedral to transact his business, he meets "a prebendary friend of mine, a man of good family, of great and superior qualities, very worthy of esteem, who was in high dudgeon because without cause men who could in no way be compared to him were taking offence at his absences" (I,222). In view of the author's appearance before the diocesan authorities in Málaga to answer similar charges, it is difficult not to see the "friend" of Marcos as Espinel himself. For Marcos then to offer advice based upon steadfastness and turning the other cheek creates a schizophrenic effect. The description of Ronda, at the end of *Descanso* xx, illustrates the same mirage technique. Marcos, speaking as from the vantage point of 1572, takes the historian Ambrosio de Morales to task for confusing Munda, the Roman name for Ronda, with Monda, a village on the slopes of the Sierra Bermeja, in his *Corónica general de España (General Chronicle of Spain)* of 1578 and reports having seen, "in the year eighty-six" (I,250), evidence of Munda having been a Roman colony. The first might be related to the time-scale of the *humilladero* conversation; the second cannot be so explained.

These novelistic tricks, although not fully or consistently exploited, give a surprisingly modern slant to *Marcos de Obregón* and contrast with the conventional nature of the episodes in which the hero is involved. Some, like the confidence trick played on the merchants by the gamblers and the recovery of the money, or Marcos' unmasking of a thief by the use of red ochre and a bell, might have their origins in the Italian short story or the popular one-act *pasos* or *entremeses* (humorous short plays) of the day; others, such as Marcos' encounters with stubborn mules and aggressive snakes, or his disastrous use of a cat-call outside the house of a Biscayan lady, have the flavor of tales told in the salons and dining-rooms of the rich acquaintances of Espinel; yet others, like the story of the priest who put "Alleluyas" into the requiem mass or of the gypsies who manage to change the look of a stolen mule but not its basic character, were well-known jokes repeated in miscellanies, novels, and plays. Only perhaps the account of the disease-stricken expeditionary force gathered in Santander has the gripping quality of eye-witness reporting, together with the tales about Ronda where the reader may feel that local patriotism adds zest to the narrative.

This section of the novel rambles amiably but aimlessly on from place to place. The disquisitions on the dog as man's best friend, the value of fatherly advice, the evils of loquacity and gambling provide the thread of teaching which is interwoven with the entertainment of the episodes to conform with Espinel's Horatian view of the aims of literature. The leisurely pace is varied by peaks of excitement — when Marcos, for example, fights for his life in the mill-race or struggles with the envious young blade he has pushed overboard in Santander harbor — and by moments of descriptive power, as when Espinel paints a word-picture of the ugliness of the innkeeper's wife at Ventas Nuevas or of the countryside around Málaga. There are also occasional flashes of humor as when Marcos rids himself of the inveterate talker by out-talking him or hints ironically at the Jewish descent of an admirer by sarcastically describing her as a "bacon-lover" (I,271) after she had thrown his present of partridges in a latrine because they were basted with bacon. As Espinel reminds the reader toward the end of this section, aware perhaps that his narrative lacked the drama and urgency that comes from dealing with great events or grand passions: ". . . here are not recorded the deeds of nobles and brave generals but rather the life of a poor squire who must endure these things and others of a similar kind" (I,269).

VIII *Valladolid: Service with the Count of Lemos*

Marcos' period of service in the household of the Count of Lemos in Valladolid straddles the first and second *relación* and covers the period from 1576 to 1578, the year of the coronation of Henry I of Portugal, following the death of Sebastian at the Battle of Alcazarquivir (supposedly foreshadowed by the comet mentioned in the text). Espinel's fulsome praise of the sixth Count of Lemos and the references to national events which link Marcos' service to a particular time lend support to the idea that Espinel is once again grafting his own experience onto that of his creation. The confusion in the text between the names of the sixth and seventh Counts of Lemos, Don Fernando and Don Pedro, may have arisen because of the time-lag between the years described (1576–78) and the period of composition (1614–16) when the seventh Count was rising forty and known as the great Maecenas of Spain, patron of Lope and Cervantes.[11] Flattery of contemporaries was common in the literature of the day as a means of currying favor, bathing in reflected glory and indicating that one was a member of a particular group. Espinel, in *Marcos de Obregón,* is not slow to use this custom for his own purposes. In the case of the Count of Lemos, however, his praise of a noble family known to be generous in its support of the arts might simply have been a way of drawing attention to himself as a deserving case. At all events, for the nobility to appear flatteringly portrayed in the pages of a novel gave a certain cachet to the author and his subject.

Marcos' openly admiring attitude toward the Count of Lemos contrasts with the *pícaros'* relationship with noble masters. Lazarillo begs for himself and for the Squire whose claim to nobility is as empty as the false code of honor to which he dedicates his life; Guzmán acts as page and procurer for the French Ambassador and himself lays claim to nobility on the strength of ill-gotten gains; Pablos' paranoiac desire to escape from his past causes him to cultivate the acquaintance of Don Diego Coronel and later to masquerade as a noble himself, only to be shamefully exposed. None of these complex motivations attach to Marcos' discreetly distanced attachment to the Count. He admires his Solomon-like judgments and his sense of humor, and, if he finds cruelty in the way he punishes gossips or laughs at the jokes played on a midget, he does not say so. Marcos does, however, permit himself a sly, ironic smile at the expense of the nobility when he admits his difficulty in first adjusting to the demands of service in the houses of the great and the need to remain constantly cheerful and alert to the demands of the master. He fears he lacks the essential qualities: "to praise wittily, add spice to a lie, bring forward softly and artfully an obsequious piece of tittle-tattle, feign friendship, hide hatred; for such things ill-befit hearts which are innocent and free" (I,274). Marcos hastens to add that, of course, the Count of Lemos is such a perfect master that his task was made much easier, a piece of social hypocrisy that shows he learned his lesson well.

The central episode in the Valladolid period is an encounter with a dwarf obsessed with the idea of becoming taller and, therefore, an easy butt for practical jokers. Marcos' involvement arises because the dwarf is convinced by his tormentors that the Squire has magical powers. Espinel is careful to make the dwarf a ridiculous figure with his absurdly high cork soles, his gyrations to keep on the same level as those with whom he is talking and his fraudulent pretensions to nobility. He is thus able to combine jokes about the midget's ability to make himself invisible by hiding behind a mosquito with high-minded platitudes about not interfering with the ways of Nature and how *hombres de bien* like Marcos — and his father before him — always consider the likely result of their actions before committing themselves and thus do not indulge in hurtful *burlas* (pranks) which could rebound and discredit them. Marcos is not able, however, to prevent "four men of good cheer" (I,280) from playing tricks on the dwarf aimed at persuading him he has grown as a result of the absurdly undignified remedies they impose upon him. The dwarf is so upset by the strange diet and so scared by the apparition of four "ghosts" as part of this treatment that he defecates. The Count, who obviously does not feel the same about cruel humor as he does about gossip, greatly enjoys a joke which has to be seen against the background of seventeenth-century taste and of a world in which, as in a Velázquez canvas, the function of dwarfs and jesters is to provide amusement, often at the sacrifice of their dignity and integrity, for the aristocracy.

IX   *Transition: The* Humilladero

The appearance of the hermit in the final *descanso* of the first *relación* and again at the beginning of the second serves to remind the reader of the situation: these reminiscences, which have taken us from Marcos' childhood in the 1550's in Ronda to his service with the Count of Lemos in the late 1570's, are being recounted in the roadside chapel near the bridge known as the Puente de Segovia in Madrid. The time-sequence of Marcos' memories is thus co-existent with another temporal scale: that of the storm and the day which has been taken up with narrating the first *relación*. As Marcos finishes his account of the way the Count deals with gossips, the hermit begins to nod and yawn with tiredness. The two take a light supper and settle down for the night.

Although the storm has abated by the morning, the height of the flood water makes it impossible for Marcos to leave the shelter of the chapel. In the introduction to the second *relación* and in the first *descanso*, Espinel takes the opportunity to put a little flesh on the bones of the shadowy figure of the hermit, to spice a homily on dreams with an anecdote about the Marquis of las Navas and to justify his protagonist's prolixity by reference to Classical theories on the aims of literature. The hermit who, on their first meeting, had claimed acquaintance with Marcos in Seville, Flanders, and Italy, now emerges as a sad figure, tormented by dreams and troubled by the loneliness of his life as a hermit. After — but, presumably, not because of — his marathon session as audience for Marcos' reminiscences and philosophizing, we are told he went to live a quiet life in Seville. Certainly, at the beginning of the second *relación*, Marcos is at pains to assure his reader that the hermit, far from being tired of his story, urged him to continue. Espinel, as author, is keen that his Squire should not be thought a prosing old fool, no better than the *habladores* (compulsive talkers) he has previously condemned. His aim is to recount events "in the plain and simple fashion that they happened, without gilding or detracting from it" (II,15). The hermit praises his sweet and graceful style of narration and, in a passage important for our knowledge of Espinel's literary aims, already quoted in Chapter III, the author criticizes the lack of continuity in a discourse, emphasizing the Horatian aim of combining instruction and entertainment, the concept of purity of language, and the need for relevance. Espinel's artistic objectives being thus reaffirmed at the beginning of the second *relación*, he allows Marcos to continue telling the story of his life.

X *Seville*

The coronation of Henry I in Lisbon in August, 1578, the epidemic which particularly affected the south of Spain from late 1580 until well into 1581, and the departure of the Duke of Medina-Sidonia in that year to take up his appointment as Governor of Milan are the verifiable events which constitute the temporal framework of Marcos' Seville period. The links with known aspects, of Espinel's life and the obvious familiarity with the layout, customs, and atmosphere of the city make it entirely feasible that, in these chapters at the beginning of the second *relación*, the author is basing himself upon his own experience. At one point in the narrative, as on many other occasions in *Marcos*, Espinel breaks the illusion of Marcos remembering his Seville days as he takes shelter from the storm in the roadside chapel by jumping from the period 1578–81 to the moment of writing. In the midst of some observations about the way justice is meted out by a judge, he comments: "The one who now holds the same office . . . Justino de Chaves . . . would not act so" (II,37). The law officer referred to was based in Seville around 1615.

Seville was often described in the literature of the Golden Age as a latter-day Babylon whose charm had become somewhat tarnished because of the vice and corruption which bred in the port chiefly associated with the gold and silver shipments from South America. Espinel's earlier visit almost certainly produced the "Satire on the Ladies of Seville," in addition to the beginnings of his reputation as a poet and musician. It also made him guiltily aware of the fatal attraction of a city which offered so many opportunities for mischief to the idler. The chapters now under consideration offer an example of the dangers of *ociosidad* (idleness) in a corrupt city. As Marcos observes: "I was in Seville some time, living night and day in a state of turmoil, with quarrels and enmities, the consequences of idleness which is the root of vice and the graveyard of virtue" (II,44). His running battle with the swaggering rogue whom he outsmarts in an encounter in the street is an illustration. Marcos foils the attempt of the bully's mistress to imprison him in her wine cellar by setting fire to it and escaping by being hauled up in a well-bucket, but he is then pursued by the law as an arsonist. By disguising himself as an invalid beggar, Marcos again escapes, this time carried on the back of one of the rascally constables sent to take him into custody. In spite of the protection first of the Marquis of Algaba and subsequently of the Marquis of Denia, later to become Duke of Lerma, Seville becomes too hot for Marcos, and he begins to ponder on the injustice which masquerades as justice and the perils which beset the idler in Seville. Thus he decides to enter the service of the Duke of Medina-Sidonia and accompany him to Italy.

It is noticeable, however, that this brush with the seamy side of life in Seville finishes in a rosy glow of self-justification. Marcos' tricks have triumphed, corruption has been exposed, and the hero finishes with a better position and in better moral shape than when he started. He is not like Lazarillo who goes from bad to worse, first in material, then in moral terms; nor is he like Pablos who disintegrates as he becomes embroiled in a hostile society. From the vantage point of old age, Marcos exudes self-righteousness.

One flaw in Espinel's system for writing his memoirs through the eyes of Marcos is a lack of selectivity. When you are making a novel not out of great events but out of *menudencias* (trifles), it is difficult to keep the forward momentum and the sense of shape. There arises a conflict between two artistic principles, both of which Espinel quotes, on occasion, with approval. The first is the Classical idea of a work of art being a well-proportioned whole, like the human body in the harmonious arrangement of its parts; the second is a precept enunciated by Renaissance theorists that art should imitate Nature in its variety. Golden Age novelistic practice was directed toward reconciling these two concepts. In the Seville chapters in *Marcos de Obregón*, we have a minor example of the failure to do so, arising perhaps out of Espinel's desire to make his Squire's memoirs a potpourri of adventures, personal reminiscence, moralizing, flattery of the famous, and amusing anecdotes. Thus, as Marcos flees to the Alameda after setting fire to the wine cellar, he comes across a cat and a snake fighting in a bush. The cat's victory causes Marcos to think more kindly of an animal he previously disliked, but it is difficult to see what this excursion into the world of the La Fontaine fable has to do with the matter in hand. Equally irrelevant are the anecdotes about the Portuguese which stem from Marcos' meeting with soldiers on their way back from the disastrous Battle of Al-cazarquivir. These stories serve to show off Espinel's command of the language and to give examples of the wit of the Portuguese; but as though aware of the risk of boring the reader and of losing the thread of the narrative, Espinel abruptly cuts short the list with the comment: "I could produce other most excellent stories and witti-cisms which, in order to avoid prolixity, I am leaving out" (II,47). In weaving his novelistic tapestry from many different threads, Espinel occasionally, as here, pauses to justify his protagonist's long-windedness when he might have been better occupied shaping his material so that Nature's variety did not clash with the principle of Classical proportions.

XI *Captivity in Algiers*

The remaining chapters of the second *relación* cover Marcos' cap-ture by pirates, the adventures which befall him during his captivity in Algiers, and his eventual escape to Genoa. The previous Seville sequence was characterized by its credibility in terms of its links with Espinel's own experience; the African adventure, by contrast, is closer to the world of fiction and, in particular, to the so-called Moorish novels popular at the time. Modern critics take issue with Pérez de Guzmán who, as evidence for taking the captivity as autobiographical, points to the wealth of detail in Espinel's description of Algiers and its customs. Closely examined, this local color turns out to consist of thinly disguised Spanish customs, such as the St. John's Day parade and tournament, and references to places in and around Algiers which could well have come from travelers' tales, Moorish fiction or from contemporary works, on North Africa, such as Luis de Mármol Carvajal's *Descripción general de Africa (General Description of Africa)* or, more particularly, Diego de Haedo's *Topographia e historia general de Argel (Topography and General History of Algiers)*. [12] In addition, the pattern of events, the situations and characters of Marcos' captivity are part of the stock-in-trade of the Moorish tradition in sixteenth- and seventeenth-century Spanish literature. Parallels have been found with Gil Polo's *La Diana enamorada (Diana in Love)*, with Lope de Vega's *Los Ponces de Barcelona*, with Ginés Pérez de Hita's *Guerras civiles de Granada*, and most of all, with Cervantes' *Don Quixote* and a number of his *Novelas ejemplares (Exemplary Novels)* and plays. Cervantes, of course, had the advantage of being able to combine his personal experience as a captive with the prevailing literary tradition; Espinel is more likely to have been working from secondary sources. Certainly no document or reference has been found which attests to his captivity, and it is unlikely that either Espinel or his contemporaries would not have capitalized on such a mark of distinction as falling into the hands of the infidel.

A curious aspect of the episode, which tends to support the idea that, in describing Marcos' experiences in captivity, Espinel was abandoning fictionalized autobiography and entering the realm of fantasy is the way in which the beginning and the end of this interlude are marked by changes in pace and direction. It is as though the reader is being to asked to step into Wonderland or through the Looking Glass and then back into normality. At the beginning, for instance, after following a usual route up the coast from Sanlúcar and then swinging out to sea toward the Balearics, the fleet in which Marcos is sailing is hit by a sudden storm which, in a remarkably short time, drives it across the Mediterranean to southern France and back to the Balearic Islands again. Such storms, in the idealistic fiction of the day, often herald fantastic adventures; Dr. Sagredo's

Byzantine exploits in South American waters are similarly prefaced
by a storm later in the novel.

The ship puts in at the island of Cabrera, and there, as it were,
the enchantment begins. Marcos and a friend find a cave, a *locus
amoenus*, cool, sweet-smelling, and with a spring of clear water
which, in its passage, has carved figures in the rock, imitating, as
does this episode itself within the framework of the novel, the variety of Nature. It is from this Wonderland that they are taken by the
pirates. At the end of his servitude in Algiers, Marcos is taken back
to the Balearics by his renegade Christian master and falls into the
hands of Marcello Doria, brother of Gian Andrea Doria in whose
galleon he originally set sail from Sanlúcar. At first his captors mistake him for the renegade, but when one of the musicians on board
sings a gloss on Espinel's own: "The doubtful good, the sure and
certain evil", a line from his "Satire on the Ladies of Seville," Marcos makes a comment and is recognized by Francisco de la Peña as
the author and composer of the piece. When Marcello Doria asks
him his name, he answers: "Marcos de Obregón," but Peña inter-
jects with: "So-and-so is his proper name, for since he comes in such
straits, he must disguise it" (II,123). Apart from some uncertainty
about Marcos' age, the African interlude is largely free of the identity game which Espinel plays with the reader throughout the earlier part of the novel. Now, as Marcos emerges from his excursion
into the sentimentalized world of Moorish fiction, Espinel gives a
sign by this curious exchange that we are back to the ambivalent
juxtaposition of the real world of the author and the fictional world of
Marcos. From this point on, Marcos takes up his route to Milan
where he left off and we are back to normal.

The details of the voyage before and after the captivity are typical
of the way Espinel embellishes lived experience in order to entertain and teach his reader. Details of the look-out system operating
along the coast to warn of the approach of pirates, information about
the Pillars of Hercules, and a display of knowledge about the rigging
and handling of ships are interwoven with lively storm scenes in
which friars vomit over sailors confessing their sins, a monkey is lost
at sea, a parrot shouts abuse from the yard-arm, the crew gets
drunk, and the boatswain hangs from the rigging by his beard.
Characteristically, Espinel uses the tribulations of the voyage, both
on the way to Cabrera and after his release, to emphasize a central
theme in the novel: *paciencia*, in this case, the will to bear with

fortitude the hardships of the storm and the later ill-treatment at the hands of the sailors who think they have caught the renegade.

The twin objectives of entertainment and instruction are, of course, central to Espinel's purpose throughout the work. The Moorish episode, almost a *sine qua non* in the idealistic fiction of the day, is only exceptional in that the entertainment offered is based upon fantasy, imagination, and literary tradition, rather than arising out of Espinel's experience; and the instruction has a noticeable element of religious propaganda. Marcos is fortunate to be captured by a renegade from Valencia who still harbors respect for the customs and religion of Spain. Taken on as tutor, Marcos becomes the object of the adoring glances of the renegade's daughter. To relieve her melancholy and frustration, the Squire devises a scheme, reminiscent of his later career as an *ensalmador*, whereby he persuades the parents to allow him to whisper "magic" words to Alima to cure her. This device, though successful in giving Marcos and the daughter opportunities to declare their affection for each other, also gives Marcos an embarrassing reputation for curing melancholia, a reputation futher enhanced when sweet words and music also cure a matron of the city. These scenes, particularly the ones with Alima in the presence of the parents, are reminiscent of deception scenes in comedies by Lope de Vega, Tirso de Molina, and Calderón. All the time, Marcos, with the father turning a blind eye, is indoctrinating the daughter and the son in the Christian faith so that, when the time comes for Marcos to win his release by his cleverness, the two children are in the frame of mind to abandon Algiers for Spain and the true religion, as they later prove in a recognition scene in the best Aristotelian tradition, a scene which offers further evidence that the Moorish interlude is a fictional sequence rather than factually based. Alima's longing for baptism is also a common feature of this type of fiction. Other examples are to be found in the Captive's tale in *Don Quixote* and in Cervantes' *Los baños de Argel (The Bagnios of Algiers)*.

The way in which Marcos obtains his release is also more appropriate in the pages of a novel than representative of true experience. The renegade offers the tutor money and his freedom if, with his well-known reputation as a schemer, he can devise a way to let the king know that the person responsible for stealing from the treasury is his own vizier. Marcos saves innocent captives from being blamed and the city from reprisals by training a thrush to say: "Hazén stole the money" and releasing it in the mosque while the king is at prayer. On the way home, the renegade, in answer to Marcos' urging to return to the faith, relates the story of the wife of Mami Reys, a former Christian captive, who after a number of years apparently happily adjusted to her new way of life, made her escape with much booty. Again, the source is probably literary since the story is similar, in its general lines, to that of *La gran Sultana (The Great Sultan's Wife)* and *El amante liberal (The Generous Lover)* by Cervantes, the latter work also supplying a possible model for Espinel's renegade in Mahamut.

This lively series of episodes is combined with moralizing passages which help to vary the pace of the narrative and relate the action to the pattern of ideas which weaves in and out of the events of the work and constitutes Espinel's philosophy of life, the fruits of his long experience. Thus, the running theme of the Moorish interlude is patience and fortitude. Marcos urges his fellow-prisoners to bear up in their troubles, playing music to soothe them and later sharing with them the extras he earns as the result of his privileged position: "I told my companions that to appreciate good it was necessary to experience some evil and to bear this tribulation with fortitude so that it might be less" (II,59). Although as an *hidalgo* (gentleman), "son of mountain people from the valley of Cayón" (II, 60), he is not accustomed to performing menial duties, Marcos accepts the inevitable and serves his master cheerfully, sprinkling his service with homilies on honor, the evils of gossip, the friendship of kings, and a continuing debate with the renegade in defense of Catholicism. The relative positions of the renegade, forced out of Spain because he could not prove his purity of descent, and Marcos, defending the traditional position of the nobility and the Church, give their conversations a topical ring and an interest which fits in well with the rest of the story.

The "Establishment" position taken up by Marcos and the ingenuity, tolerance, and fortitude he displays as a captive are projections of the way Espinel sees himself in the role. In that sense, the Moorish episode, although based on literary models, is intended as part of the same identification process between the author and his creation which characterizes the rest of the work. Uncertainty over Marcos' age at this time supports this view. The voyage to Italy, according to the chronology already established, belongs to the year 1581, when Espinel and his creation were thirty-one. Marcos is capable of feeling a passion for Alima he was incapable of feeling for Doña Mergelina de Aybar, wife of Dr. Sagredo, and yet he describes himself to the girl as "weighed down with age" (II,78). A little later, in Italy, Marcos appears as "very young and with a taste for new experiences" (II,150). It is as though the chain of cross-references between Marcos and Espinel is broken by this entry into a Moorish fantasy and the author is unclear about the age of his creation, thinking of him now as a young man capable of attracting the renegade's daughter, now as an old man exercising that gift for curing by spells which he has as a charity pensioner at the beginning of the work. A similar apparent lack of sureness of touch is shown when, on the occasion of the St. John's Day tournament, Marcos is describing such an event in the Spanish capital and seizes the opportunity, on behalf of his creator, to mention flatteringly the nobles who took part.[13] The hermit interrupts to ask why he does not mention the tourney held by Philip III in Valladolid in 1605 to celebrate the birth of his son. Marcos replies: "Because I was not about to recount prophetically what had not yet happened" (II, 91–92). He then goes on to describe the fiesta, naming further nobles and praising the horsemanship of the King himself. Yet it is only from the vantage point of 1614–16, the time when Marcos was supposedly writing his memoirs in the pensioners' home of Santa Catalina de los Donados, that the Valladolid celebration of 1605 can be viewed in retrospect. The meeting with the hermit belongs to the 1580's. These anachronisms are both a strength and a weakness of *Marcos de Obregón*. They are a strength because the resulting difference of points of view adds an extra dimension, a feeling of hindsight to the novel as the old author projects his experience and philosophy on to his younger fictional self; they are a weakness because their random distribution can give an impression of carelessness and inconsistency in the handling of the time zones of the novel.

XII *Transition: The Third* Relación

In the transition between the second and the third *relación*, there is no return to the scene of Marcos' reminiscences: the roadside chapel, the flood waters in the wake of the storm, and the hermit politely fighting off tiredness and encouraging Marcos to continue the story of his life. Instead, the introduction to the *relación* continues where the last chapter left off with adventures befalling the Squire on his trip from Genoa to take up his post in Milan. Caught in a torrential downpour, Marcos and his mule-boy eventually find food and shelter in a remote house, where the hero's liking for cold water causes consternation to his host and sparks off a disquisition on the poor quality of Italian water, in which snakes and all manner of nasty creatures breed, compared to the excellence of the water from various parts of Spain, particularly Marcos-Espinel's native Ronda. The Squire points out: ". . . in all the time I was in Lombardy, which was more than three years, I never enjoyed good health nor was I free from a continual headache, because of the water I drank" (II,129). This comment, confirmed by a later reference to "three years" (II,144) spent in Milan, helps to fix the period spent in Italy as from 1581 to 1584, which coincides with the biography of the author who left for Italy in the retinue of the Duke of Medina-Sidonia toward the end of April, 1581 and, on the evidence of his poetic activity, was back in Madrid in 1584. It is also interesting to note, from this introduction, that the wet climate of northern Italy and the contaminated water seem not to have suited either the protagonist or his creator and, later in life, Espinel seems to have blamed his declining health and his worsening gout on this period.

XIII *The Italian Experience*

Marcos' Italian period, which occupies rather less than half of the third *relación*, is a composite of Espinel's experiences, in some cases verifiable by reference to external sources, together with travelers' tales and episodes chiefly modeled upon the popular theater and the Italian short-story collections of the day. A moral commentary arising out of the incidents provides a unifying strand which binds together the different phases of the narration. Thus, sermonizing on greed, astrology, honor, and the position of the Spaniard abroad is interwoven around autobiographical and fictional incidents varying from the scatologically farcical when Marcos escapes from drowning by hanging on to his horse's tail to the Gothic horror of Aurelio's punishment of his wife's supposed adultery.

Traveling from Genoa to Milan, Marcos takes the regular route, probably the one followed by Espinel himself, through San Pier d'Arena, Alessandria della Paglia, across the Po to Pavia, and on to his destination. In Milan, fact and fiction come together when Mar-

cos, as "author of this book" (II,143), is commisioned to write elegiac
verses in connection with the service to be held in the cathedral in
September, 1581 to commemorate the death in the previous year of
Ana de Austria, fourth wife of Philip II. These poems — three
sonnets and a *canción* which was not in fact used — appeared later
in Espinel's *Miscellaneous Verse*.[14] That same month, the Dowager
Empress María, mother of the late Queen, visited Milan on her way
from Vienna to enter a convent in Spain. In describing the ceremonial of her reception, Marcos gives the impression of seeing the
event through Espinel's eyes. The novelist was, after all, in Milan at
that time and enjoyed the protection of Ottavio Gonzaga, who
commanded the cavalry mentioned in the passage. For some
reason, however, Espinel departs from the historical sequence of
events by interposing Marcos' visit to Turin between the obsequies
and the State visit. Also in question in this section is Marcos-
Espinel's presence in Flanders. At the beginning of *Descanso* iv, on
his return from Turin, Marcos mentions his intention to go to Flanders. He decides against it, partly because he had already been at
the Battle of Maestricht. Pérez de Guzmán and Calabritto take the
view that it was at this battle that Espinel first met Ottavio Gonzaga.
It is more likely, however, that the author was in Seville in 1579 (see
Chapter I) and that the two became acquainted in Italy, where
Espinel wrote the poems addressed to Gonzaga and his wife which
appear in *Miscellaneous Verse*. Much has been made, too, of the
reference to Antonia Calatayud (II,178) which occurs in this section.
Some commentators have attempted, on the basis of this single
mention, to equate her with the Célida of the love poems of *Miscellaneous Verse*. The evidence is flimsy, and some care must obviously be exercised not only in establishing the facts of Espinel's life
but also in equating the details of that life with those of his
fictionalized self. The contradictions in Marcos' age during the Italian episode are a further indication of the need for care. When he
goes to see the necromancer he is a "young lad" (II, 150); by the
time he has reached Marseilles three years later, he is "around fifty"
(II,202). The account of Marcos' musical life in Milan, however, can
be more readily accepted as corresponding with the author's own
experience. Marcos anachronistically compares the soirées in the
house of Antonio de Londoño with similar gatherings of the friends
of Bernardo Clavijo taking place "these days" (II,156) in Madrid,
i.e., at the time of composition of the novel, not at the time of

talking to the hermit. Marcos' observations on musical theory and his anecdote about the lover who tried to imitate the tragedy of Espinel's own "Break the veins of the passionate breast" have the ring of remembered truth. On Marcos' journey home we may be skeptical about the autobiographical nature of Marcos' adventures at sea, but the mention of Fernando de Toledo, who at the beginning of the novel features as an example of good-humored forbearance and who has an eclogue dedicated to him in the collected verse miscellany, is further evidence that the events in Italy, in their general lines and sequence, follow Espinel's own path.

Some of the picturesque incidents which befall Marcos in Italy, such as being stoned by peasants, being sunk in the Po and pulling himself out by his horse's tail, or ingeniously using a leather wine bottle and an inflated doublet to save himself from drowning off Marseilles, could pass as travelers' tales, loosely based on Espinel's experience. In the main, however, the author has grafted onto the framework of his visit to Italy material which seems to become progressively more literary as the sequence unfolds. At first, when Marcos escapes from prison by an alchemist's trick which exploits the greed of his jailor, we are moving in the world of the short plays of Cervantes or Lope de Rueda or the more popular type of Italian short story. Marcos' unmasking of the necromancer's use of a magnet to deceive the gullible Swiss is also in the same vein. Both episodes exploit the popular interest in the "black arts" frowned upon by the Church. The Venetian adventures, however, which take up *Descansos* vi–ix of this final *relación*, belong to a different and somewhat decadent world of aristocrats and courtesans in which bloody revenge masquerades as honor, and hospitality is a front for the confidence trick. Aurelio and Camila, the central characters in the two episodes, represent two different aspects of the Boccaccian short story: tragic passion, which is allied to the taste for spectacular acts of revenge, and feminine trickery. Critics have found analogues in the work of other Italian writers of the period — Ariosto, for example, in the introductory section of the Aurelio sequence and Sacchetti for the Camila story —, but the basic inspiration is undoubtedly Boccaccio's *Decameron*. Espinel is here seen capitalizing on his familiarity with the Italian fictional scene.[15]

The interesting thing about Espinel's treatment of this material, however, is the way in which he uses Marcos as a catalyst to change the tone and course of events. In the case of Aurelio, the initial presentation of the melancholy hunter, falcon on his wrist, who invites a suspicious Marcos, who has been abandoned by his mule-boy, to shelter for the night in his stark and gloomy mansion has an Italianate "feel" about it and prepares us for the "sad story and frightful spectacle" (II,176) which is to come. After dinner, Aurelio tells Marcos his story of a happy marriage and a peaceful life dedicated to hunting blighted by the treachery of his squire Cornelio whom he suspects of having an affair with his wife while he is away on his trips. At first, he is content to keep Cornelio with him to restrict his opportunities, but the squire then begins to masquerade as a ghost to lure the husband away from the bedroom. Setting a trap for Cornelio, Aurelio discovers a secret way into his wife's room, the entrance to which is symbolically covered by a painting of the adultery of Venus and Mars. Cornelio breaks his legs in trying to escape and the husband garrottes him. Aurelio also kills the servant who witnessed the affair, but when he tries to stab his wife he finds, like García del Castañar in Rojas Zorrilla's *Del rey abajo, ninguno,* that his hand is mysteriously restrained. He therefore decides to starve her to death, with the body of her supposed lover for company and his dismembered heart set between them. This is the scene which, two weeks later, confronts Marcos at the end of Aurelio's account. In commenting, Marcos reveals a humane attitude toward honor akin to that displayed by Cervantes and Tirso de Molina. Not for Marcos-Espinel the Calderonian wife-murder or Lope's exquisitely cruel "punishment without vengeance." For Marcos, the important factors are: Aurelio's undoubted love for his wife, revealed by the story of their first meeting and his emotion at the sight of her distress; the need for secrecy; and the circumstantial nature of the evidence against a previously blameless wife. Aurelio, in killing Cornelio and the servant who exaggerated the seriousness of the affair, has punished the guilty and ensured secrecy. Therefore, Marcos reasons, honor is satisfied, and Aurelio, accepting his advice, is reunited with his wife. In urging mercy and love, Marcos emerges as a man of balanced judgment and humane instincts, giving a different twist to this Italianate story of bloody revenge. Espinel thus joins the large group of writers who, echoing popular opinion, soften the harsh outlines of the Honor Code in the Golden Age. In changing the course of events in this story, however, Espinel does not lessen the tension. He cleverly underlines the symbolism of the heart as a source of life and death by linking Aurelio's

account of when he first saw his wife: ". . . it happened one day
that, as I went hunting with a falcon on one hand and a heart in the
other for bait, my own [heart] was torn from me, leaving implanted
in it an idea which has neither been effaced nor will it ever be"
(II,164), with the horrific dénouement of the bodies, the heart of
Cornelio, and the dogs licking their dying mistress. Espinel does
not linger over the horror of the scene, but in a few masterly
painter's strokes indicates to us why he enjoys a reputation for descriptive power rare among Golden Age writers.

Marcos' intervention also changes the course of the Camila story.
What starts as a tale to illustrate feminine wiles finishes as an example of the biter bitten. The courtesan poses as Aurelio's sister-in-law
charged with entertaining Marcos in Venice, a city whose inhabitants, Marcos tells us, are as vain as the Portuguese. The Squire
then goes on to show how, by answering deception with deception,
Marcos triumphs over the vain confidence trickster. In an atmosphere reminiscent of one of María de Zayas' feminist tales, Camila
tricks Marcos into keeping his papers and the gifts he received from
Aurelio in a casket to which she has the key. When she steals it,
Marcos, in his turn tricks the courtesan into releasing the casket by
means of a forged bond which he purports to wish to cash but lacks
the necessary identification papers. This lively example of Greek
meeting Greek has the picaresque flavor of those representatives of
the genre with female protagonists, such as López de Ubeda's *La
pícara Justina* or Castillo Solórzano's *La niña de los embustes (The
Girl with the Tricks)*, but the triumph of Marcos and his plea of
self-defense at the end indicate the gulf which lies between *Marcos
de Obregón* and the picaresque genre in general.

XIV   *Back in Madrid*

The central section of the third *relación* takes us up to the point
where Marcos leaves the service of the Sagredos and should, therefore, take his leave of the hermit. As was pointed out in Section IV of
this chapter, however, through an oversight or a printer's error, that
leavetaking has been transposed to the end of the work with the
result that the chronology goes haywire. In discussing this part of
the work, we shall correct the time-sequence by considering the
relevant paragraph from *Descanso* xxv where it properly belongs, at
the end of *Descanso* xiii.

Marcos' return from Italy to Madrid in about 1584 is, at first, a happy one. Like his creator, he finds friends eager to welcome him back and hear of his experiences and an aristocratic master to serve. The evidence of Espinel's biography would lead us to believe that the circle of friends alluded to are the writers Cervantes, Lope de Vega, Liñán de Riaza and Pedro de Padilla. They all contributed dedicatory verses, along with Espinel, to Juan López Maldonado's *Cancionero* of 1586, and the whole group was included in Espinel's valedictory "The House of Memory." The noble master referred to may have been either the Marquis of Peñafiel, to whom Espinel directed an epistle in *Miscellaneous Verse* or, more likely, the Duke of Alba to whom the whole collection is dedicated. The latter could have employed the writer on the recommendation of his kinsman, Fernando de Toledo with whom Marcos came into contact on his way home and who is mentioned elsewhere in *Marcos de Obregón* in flattering terms. There is also a link between the obesity and gout which afflict both Espinel and his Squire. The doctors who, in 1594, testified to Espinel's unfitness to travel to Ronda to answer charges of dereliction of duty, stated that they had been treating him for ten years, that is to say, since the period of Marcos' return to Madrid. At this point in the novel, Marcos does not blame his ill-health on the after-effects of Italy but rather upon the comfortable life with his new master. He succumbs to his old enemy, idleness, and suffers the inevitable consequences for one of his constitution: "Idle loafing beset me and I became so fat that gout began to make a martyr of me" (II,206).

The consequences of idleness are highlighted by the whole of this Madrid section. Not only does Marcos, like his creator, become obese and gout-ridden as a result of good living, he also begins to feel unsettled and restless, which causes him to fall out of favor with his aristocratic master. Since the latter neglects him, he begins to wander idly about Madrid in the evenings with a friend. During one of these outings, as the result of a race foolishly undertaken for a bet, they are wrongfully arrested as escaping felons and imprisoned. On his release, Marcos is approached for advice by a gentleman who cannot eat or sleep. The Squire diagnoses idleness and takes the gentleman for a long walk, ostensibly in search of herbs to cure his condition. After the exercise the man eats a hearty meal and sleeps like a log. Marcos does not fail to point the moral of these incidents, illustrating the dangers of over-eating with the fable of the mouse who eats the canary's seed and than cannot get through the bars of the cage and prescribing, in his own case and that of the *caballero*, a frugal diet and plenty of exercise.

The prison sequence, however, has a more picaresque flavor than the healthy-mindedness which surrounds it and signifies a return to the cunning Marcos who hoodwinked Camila and unmasked the necromancer. Marcos' experiences in jail are akin to those of Quevedo's Pablos, although, happily perhaps for modern taste, without the vomit and excrement which serve to underline the *pícaro*'s degradation. Marcos and his friend share a cell with a King Rat type who terrorizes the other prisoners, "an old lag, red-haired, bad-tempered, with enormous whiskers that reached as far as his ears" (II,212). It is these whiskers, of which he is inordinately proud, which prove to be his undoing for, to humiliate him, Marcos hits on the idea of cutting off one half of his moustache while he is asleep, leaving him like a "Herculean bull with one horn missing" (II,213). This incident is vividly described, but again, the differences between *Marcos de Obregón* and the picaresque genre are emphasized. Espinel tempers his social criticism of the administration of justice with careful diplomacy and causes Marcos to appear mealy-mouthed as he justifies the prank by which the bully was cut down to size.

There is a curious incident as Marcos and his friend leave prison after three months. As they are attempting to sell their belongings to get a fresh start, a gentleman purporting to be acting for another who admires their fortitude offers them money to compensate for their time in jail. Marcos recognizes him as the real culprit in the affray which led to their arrest. Marcos indicates to the *hidalgo* that his guilt is known; the *hidalgo*, in his turn, shows that he knows Marcos to be responsible for cutting off the bully's moustache. The protagonist decides to take the proffered money, give up his hated job as a squire, and leave the capital.

He does, in fact, enter the service of the Sagredos. This brings us to the beginning of the first flashback. There is then a short paragraph which summarizes Marcos' service with the Sagredos, and we are logically at the point in the Squire's second flashback where the protagonist should say goodbye to the hermit (see Section IV). Transposing the relevant paragraph from *Descanso* xxv, we find the hermit, "perhaps tired from having listened to me for so long" (II, 306), indicating that the flood waters have receded sufficiently for the bridge to be passable. Marcos leaves his confidant and crosses the Manzanares, surveying the wreckage as he goes and alluding to the story, repeated by other Golden Age writers, that a floating saddle had been mistaken for a whale.

XV Return to Andalusia

As Marcos flees from the bustle of the capital, heading for his native Ronda, the formula Espinel uses for narrating his Squire's experiences does not change. There is still the same admixture of entertainment and enlightenment, of incidents and encounters larded with moral commentary and disquisitions on a variety of topics; there is still the same blurring of the outlines of identity between the real and supposed author. The difference, in the chapters leading up to the reappearance of Dr. Sagredo and the final curtain, is that as Espinel ties up the loose ends of the narrative and brings his protagonist home, he intensifies the identity game he has intermittently played with the reader throughout the novel, giving his creation further autonomy while, at the same time, allowing us at the end to catch a glimpse of the face behind the mask.

Starting with the types he meets at the Venta de Darazután, Marcos encounters a whole gallery of oddities in a return home which is reminiscent of Pablos going to collect his inheritance in the *Buscón (The Sharper)*: a squire whose present poverty, like that of his counterpart in the *Lazarillo*, does not match up with his distant prospects: "And if I'm on foot at the moment, it's because I have my horses out grazing in Pontedeume" (II,226); a priest who, in a passage to which the Church authorities later took exception, insists on praying out loud as he walks along; a prattling *pícaro* in the making who delights in witty ripostes. In an interpolated tale, this lad tells of his wanderings and adventures since leaving his home in Torreperogil with four coins stolen from his father. It is a picaresque novel in miniature whose protagonist, like Lazarillo, "always went from bad to worse" (II,239), his sleep on a bench being interrupted by an invasion of pigs or his thefts from the kitchen of the monastery where he had been accepted as a novice being discovered by his superiors. Always, however, he managed to survive by using his wits. At the end of the recital, the contrast in attitude between Marcos and the young *pícaro* is plain. Marcos emphasizes that, in looking after our own interests, we must ensure that it is "without harming a third party" (II,243); the rogue insists that we simply have an obligation to look after ourselves even though it be "at another's cost" (II,243), illustrating his point with an animal fable. The following morning, Marcos muses on how these clever young people are led astray by their superficial understanding of life.

Marcos' companion on the first part of his journey is a judge from Seville, Don Hernando de Villaseñor, who, apart from being a real-life character from Cañete el Real who later held high office in the central administration of the affairs of the New World, has a twofold interest in the context of the novel. In the first place, he introduces a discussion on memory which casts fascinating sidelights on Espinel's working methods in the composition of these memoirs. His talk with Marcos reflects a renewed interest in sixteenth-century Europe in mnemonics, a technique of memory by association of ideas first outlined by the Ancients. More important for *Marcos de Obregón*, however, is the line taken by Marcos in the discussion. He will have nothing to do with artificial systems nor with the sterile accumulation of remembered facts for their own sake. For him: ". . . memory is something which seems divine, for it holds past things in the here and now" (II,227). In spite of the dangers of bringing back unhappiness, memory, properly used, can be an ally of understanding. Statues, rivers, trees, and all manner of things can trigger the memory which is then, in Marcos' opinion, to be combined with Nature's gift of understanding, enriched by the reading of serious authors and contact with learned friends.

Time past and time present, linked by memory and enriched by experience: this is essentially the process which produced *Marcos de Obregón*. As Marcos records the past for his creator, the mention of a place, a person, or an incident triggers off an association, and he digresses from the mainstream of his life story to bring back from the recesses of his memory thoughts on a wide range of subjects. Indeed, the two main flashbacks themselves are inspired by "chance" references to the need for forbearance and to places from Marcos' past. The process whereby memories and apparent digressions are welded together to produce a slow-moving but richly textured novel anticipates the technique used by Proust in *A la recherche du temps perdu*.

Among many more famous examples of feats of memory, Marcos cites his own case: "The author of this book, having left his parents' house as a young student and returning with white hairs to it, knew and put a name to all those he left behind as children, as he came across them with beards and grey hair" (II,229). The obvious coincidence here between Marcos' experience and that of his creator brings us to the second point of interest in the introduction of the judge. Although we are never told why, the latter is anxious to meet Marcos de Obregón, and the protagonist poses as a great friend of his, playing the same game with the jurist as Espinel does with his reader throughout the novel by projecting another self on to a relationship. Marcos recites some verses to his companion which are fresh from his pen: "so much so that they had not passed from my hands to a second person" (II,227), and as they travel on together discussing the power of memory and mentioning examples from the past, Marcos, this time as the author of the book, talks of his return to Ronda. The judge asks the protagonist what kind of man Marcos is. Marcos replies: "The size and general appearance of his person is similar to mine and his manner and conduct, likewise; for since we are such great friends, I follow him and he, me" (II,231). And so Marcos continues, hearing good of himself, until the time comes for him to part from the judge in Cordova. When Marcos is about a hundred paces away, he cannot resist the temptation to turn and shout: ". . . I am Marcos de Obregón" (II,245). The playfulness of this episode should not blind us to its significance as part of the process whereby Espinel, like Cervantes in the *Quixote*, grants a degree of autonomy to his central character in order to produce the effect of differing levels of reality between the author, the creation, and the reader. Marcos, like Don Quixote, can discuss his fictional self; Espinel, like Cervantes, can give the impression that he enjoys an especially intimate relationship with his reader, giving him the opportunity to look over his shoulder at the act of literary creation.

The process is taken a step further still in one of the three chance encounters which occur in these chapters as Espinel ties up the loose ends of his narrative in preparation for the ending. Two of these meetings might have come from the pages of any of the Byzantine novels of adventure popular at the time. They have an air of novelistic coincidence about them, indicating that Espinel is following the Aristotelian formula for bringing together the separate elements of a novel. In the first reunion scene, Marcos is asked by Juan de Loja in Málaga to check the *bona fides* of a Moorish brother and sister who turn out to be his former charges in Algiers. They have been shipwrecked in their escape from arranged marriages to Spain and the true religion taught to them by Marcos. The chronology breaks down as they refer to the "eight years" (II,247) that have passed since the latter's departure from Algiers because other evidence would indicate that Marcos' return to Ronda coincides with the author's, i.e., *ca.* 1585, only four years after his supposed captivity. Also, at the end of *Descanso* xvi, Espinel takes over from Marcos and adopts the traditionally omniscient attitude of the author in order to round off the story of the renegade's children: "They journeyed to Valencia to make the acquaintance of the relatives of their father, where they lived with such spiritual consolation that I had word that they finished their lives as a great example of Christian virtue" (II,252). Another chance meeting is with Dr. Sagredo. Both he and Marcos independently fall into the hands of the same brigands and Sagredo, dressed not as a doctor now but in the tattered remnants of a soldier's uniform, embarks upon a tale of woe which occupies the next six *descansos.*

It is, however, the third casual encounter, with Pedro Jiménez Espinel, which sets the seal on the process whereby the novelist and his creation have shared the same identity. Coming to the Sauceda de Ronda, Marcos meets up with an old man who seems to have achieved that peace and contentment away from the noise and bustle of civilization which is associated with the name of Horace and which was so sought after in the pastoral novels and the bucolic verse of the Golden Age. The old man describes how, in his idyllic life, he is strengthened in humility and patience by the reading of Fray Luis de Granada's *Memorial de la vida cristiana (Account of the Christian Life)*, and Marcos is curious to know more about this man whose ideals so closely correspond to his own. He avoids giving his own name but when the old man gives his as "Pedro Jiménez Espinel," Marcos says: "My heart gave a thump" (II,255). Now, there is no reason for Marcos de Obregón to be startled by the mention of the name "Espinel" unless there is some connection between the protagonist and the author. Marcos later reinforces the point when replying to the old man's enquiry about a wandering nephew of his, last heard of in Italy: " 'What is his name?' I asked, and he answered me with my own name. 'Yes, I know him' I said, 'and he is the greatest friend I have in the world. He is alive and in Spain, quite close to here, where without traveling far you can see him and talk to him' " (II,256). Marcos had previously retreated behind the "best friend" mask to hide his identity from the judge; now he hides his other identity, the "Mr. So-and-so," "Mr. X," "the author of this book," about whom there has been so much playful evasion in the course of the novel. The secret is thus out; the game is over. Marcos and Espinel are revealed as one and the same, returning home to Ronda to take up a new vocation and (as is clear from early poems) hoping to find that Horatian peace and contentment which Pedro Jiménez Espinel enjoys but which both Marcos and Espinel did not find until old age when, attached to a religious institution, they settled down to distil the experience of a lifetime into the form of memoirs. The result was *Marcos de Obregón.*

XVI *The Sagredos in the New World*

As if in reaction to this moment of intimacy in the novel when Marcos meets Pedro Jiménez Espinel, the author then devotes the next six chapters (*Descansos* xix to xxiv) to an account by Marcos' former master of the fantastic adventures which befell the Sagredos on an expedition to the Straits of Magellan. As Valentín de Pedro has pointed out, however, in spite of echoes of the chivalresque and Byzantine novels, of the mythical wanderings of the *Odyssey,* and of the exaggeration of travelers' tales, the basic framework of this trip to the land of the Patagonian giants is historically accurate.[16] The expedition he describes, planned by Pedro Sarmiento de Gamboa and led by Diego Flores de Valdés, did set out from Sanlúcar in 1581, under the patronage of Philip II, to colonize, extend, and defend Spain's toehold in the Straits.

Espinel was obviously familiar with the accounts of exploration in the New World by Pigafetta, Transilvano, López de Gómara, and others since he follows the main lines of the story as given by such chroniclers: the turning back of the ships to winter in Cadiz; the first stage of the journey to Rio de Janeiro; the splitting up of the fleet; the flora and fauna of the new territory; the ill-fated attempt to establish outposts; the return of Diego Flores de Valdés with part of the original force to Spain. Onto this framework, however, Espinel builds a series of fantastic adventures which more properly belong within the pages of the idealistic fiction popular in his day: the valiant youth who, like a knight-errant, attacks the sea monster with a sword and diamond-studded shield; the race of giants on Inaccessible Island whose awesome idol is blown up by the resourceful Sagredo; the attack by Turkish pirates in the Straits of Gibraltar which leads to the presumed loss by drowning of Doña Mergelina de Aybar. And yet this curious amalgam of semi-historical account and fantastic adventure, in which Marcos has a purely passive role as a listener, is not so far removed from the major themes of the novel as might be imagined. Just as Cervantes' *El curioso impertinente* (*The Man Who Was Too Curious for His Own Good*) seems to be divorced from the concerns of Don Quixote and yet turns out to be relevant for its portrayal of the consequences of obsession, so Sagredo's deeds in the New World are a projection of Marcos' own ingenuity and resourcefulness onto the world of high adventure which neither he nor his creator managed to inhabit. As with the captivity in Algiers, Espinel, through Sagredo, is giving us the opportunity vicariously to enjoy a feeling of danger and excitement, of being involved in the pioneering days of the opening up of the New World.

The same ingenious tricks, the same courage and resource which helped Marcos to escape from many a tight spot are now attributed to Dr. Sagredo as he becomes the savior of the expedition. For example, when it seems as though the sailors will never escape from the clutches of the giants, Sagredo does not despair: "But as one must not lose one's courage in any adversity, if tribulations are the touchstone of valor and inventiveness, then it came to me how we could help ourselves in such a tight corner, to which courage, ingenuity and speed should all be applied together in a flash" (II,276). These qualities, together with the often-mentioned patience in adversity, are the ones which help to define the mood of *Marcos de Obregón*. Here Espinel is showing them being applied to a sequence of adventures and derring-do which caters for popular taste and provides an outlet for feelings of wish-fulfillment on the part of the author and the reader.

There is yet another coincidental reunion at the end of Dr. Sagredo's recital when a "very handsome little page" (II,295) falls into the hands of Roque Amador's brigands and turns out to be Sagredo's lost wife. With an appropriate pause for suspense, Doña Mergelina tells of her escape from the pirates by disguising herself as a page and her subsequent search for her husband. Marcos and the Sagredos are set free by the bandit leader and make their way to Madrid.

XVII *Epilogue*

Since we have transposed Marcos' farewell to the hermit to where it properly belongs, at the end of *Descanso* xiii, we are left with the final short chapter in which, by way of epilogue, Marcos-Espinel, tired of the buffeting of Fortune, decides to settle down and prepare for death. He defines the aim of his memoirs as an attempt, in clear and simple language, to combine instruction and entertainment. The central message, or to use a favorite metaphor of picaresque authors, the "fruit" hidden beneath the outer skin, as Espinel has already explained in his Prologue, is patience. For without that quality neither he nor his protagonist could have endured the hardships of life nor enjoyed the favor of the great; with it, they have been able to combat the dangers of idleness. As the author explains: "Keeping busy is the great teacher of patience, a virtue we should always keep our thoughts on with great vigilance in order to resist the temptations which torment us without and within" (II,309–10). The writer reinforces his championship of this typically Spanish virtue, a virtue which is more active and heroic, more akin to fortitude, than the English word "patience" allows, by citing living examples: the Duke of Osuna, who set aside the excesses of his youth and became a model Viceroy of Sicily; Jorge de Tovar who was also known early in life to be impulsive in matters of honor, later acquired the moral virtues associated with patience and served as Secretary of the Council to Philip III. It is noticeable that by the end of the novel, when the author mentions that his neighbor is the Duchess of Sessa, Espinel's disguise as Marcos, a charity pensioner at Santa Catalina de los Donados, with a local reputation for curing by spells, has been cast aside and we are listening to the accumulated wisdom of Vicente Espinel, author of *Marcos de Obregón*, chapel-master of the Capilla del Obispo which was, in effect, adjacent to the town house of the Duke of Sessa.

CHAPTER 5

Summary

VICENTE Espinel's two major compositions, the *Diversas rimas* (*Miscellaneous Verse*) and his novel, *Relaciones de la vida del escudero Marcos de Obregón* (*Account of the Life of the Squire Marcos de Obregón*) have earned for him a rather enduring claim to fame as versifier and story-teller. While his reputation as a poet was probably relatively greater among his contemporaries than indicated by today's retrospective judgments, Espinel's stature as a novelist can be said not only to be undiminished, but likely enhanced by the historical vicissitudes of the intervening centuries. The fact that all major reprintings of *Marcos de Obregón* have occurred within the last one hundred years suggests that the work enjoys greater prestige than at any time following its appearance early in the seventeenth century. A subsequent edition of the *Miscellaneous Verse* shortly after the mid-point of our century affords a basis for speculation that a re-evaluation of the historical significance of Espinel as poet may yet come about, although his lyric themes and techniques are rather far removed from the taste of the present age.

Criticism of Espinel has tended to emphasize the autobiographical (or presumably autobiographical) input both in poetry and prose, and a reflection of this is found in the biographical literature which attempts to fill the existing gaps in what is known of the writer's life by drawing — perhaps too literally — upon his creative works. In view of the essentially traditional nature of Espinel's ideology and the already indicated correspondence between salient aspects of both the poetry and prose and literary conventions of the period, the reader might well beware of an overly literal or fanciful interpretation of the seemingly personal episodes, even though the existence of obvious parallels is beyond debate and has been sketched in considerable detail in the foregoing study.

144

Of greatest interest for the student of literature and literary theory is Espinel's contribution — historically precocious in various aspects — to the aesthetic linkage between novel and autobiography, novelist and narrator, creator and personage. Anticipating, with a subtlety far ahead of his time, the modern evolution in the direction of use of literary masks, doubles, and the *alter ego*, Espinel emerges as a previously unrecognized but enormously significant antecedent of contemporary novelistic technique. He may undisputably be seen as a predecessor of the *Doppelgänger* in the European novel in general, and as foreshadowing the extensive utilization of the literary double by the Generation of '98 in Spain.

Notes and References

Chapter One

1. See Juan Pérez de Guzmán, "Vicente Espinel y su obra" in *Vida del escudero Marcos de Obregón* (Barcelona, 1881) and, more recently, Diego Vázquez Otero, *Vida de Vicente Martínez Espinel* (Málaga, 1948).

2. Joaquín de Entrambasaguas' "Datos biográficos de Vicente Espinel en sus *Diversas rimas*," *Revista Bibliográfica y Documental*, IV (1950), 171–241, illustrates this process.

3. Except where otherwise stated, this biographical sketch is based upon George Haley's fundamental study, *Vicente Espinel and Marcos de Obregón. A Life and Its Literary Representation* (Providence, Rhode Island, 1959).

4. To avoid confusion, the division of the work into *relaciones* and *descansos* has been ignored in references to textual details; the numbers given relate to the corresponding volume and page in the Gili Gaya edition (Madrid, 1960).

5. Page references to *Diversas rimas* are taken from the edition by Dorothy Clotelle Clarke (New York, 1956).

6. Published by Eugenio Mele and Adolfo Bonilla y San Martín in the *Revista de Archivos, Bibliotecas y Museos*, X (1904), 410–15, the "Sátira" is a good example of the vituperative side of Espinel's poetic talents, a side also exhibited in the verse epistle to the Marquis of Peñafiel and in other parts of *Diversas rimas (Miscellaneous Verse)* See Chapter 1, Section XV and Chapter 2, Section V.

7. *El ingenioso hidalgo don Quijote de la Mancha*, ed. Francisco Rodríguez Marín (Madrid, 1947–49), IV, 179. Subsequent references will give volume and page numbers from this edition. The passage in question is quoted in full by Haley, *op. cit.*, p. 8, n.16.

8. See Marcelino Menéndez y Pelayo, *Orígenes de la novela*, (Madrid, 1905), I, 481, n.1 and Gili Gaya, *ed. cit.*, I, 12.

9. Pellegrino de' Pellegrini's account of Espinel's part in this tribute is reproduced by Julián Zarco Cuevas, "La primera edición de unas poesías latinas y españolas de Vicente Espinel," *Boletín de la Real Academia Es-*

pañola, XVIII (1931), 91–101 and by Joaquín de Entrambasaguas, "Vicente Espinel, poeta de la reina Ana de Austria," *Revista de Literatura*, VIII (1955), 228–38 and IX (1956) 139–48.

10. Cf. *Diversas rimas, ed. cit.*, pp. 68–73 and pp. 73–77.

11. Both Juan Pérez de Guzmán and Dorothy Clotelle Clarke, in their respective introductions, give versions of the Célida affair.

12. See George Haley, "Vicente Espinel and the *Romancero General*," *Hispanic Review*, XXIV (1956), 101–14.

13. For background material on the extent and importance of literary academies in the Golden Age, see José Sánchez, *Academias literarias del Siglo de Oro español* (Madrid: Gredos, 1961) and Willard F. King, *Prosa novelística y academias literarias en el siglo XVII* (Madrid: Anejos del Boletín de la Real Academia Española*, 1963). Espinel's involvement with the Congregación de Esclavos del Santísimo Sacramento is attested by Hugo A. Rennert and Américo Castro, *Vida de Lope de Vega* (Madrid, 1919), p. 200.

14. See Haley, *Vicente Espinel and* Marcos de Obregón, p. 41.

15. J. Simón Díaz, in "Textos dispersos de clásicos españoles, IV: Espinel," *Revista de Literatura*, XVI (1959), 169–84, lists *aprobaciones* by Espinel.

16. See Francisco de Quevedo, *Vida del Buscón*, ed. Américo Castro (Madrid: Clásicos Castellanos, 1911), p. 119.

17. This quotation from Espinel's earliest known *aprobación* can be found in Haley, *op. cit.*, p. 42.

18. The case for an actual master-pupil relationship between Espinel and Lope de Vega, rebutted by Haley, p. 8, is presented by Joaquín de Entrambasaguas in *Vivir y crear de Lope de Vega* (Madrid, 1946), pp. 22–23, and in the same critic's *Estudios sobre Lope de Vega* (Madrid: C.S.I.C., 1946), I, 512–17.

19. See *Epistolario de Lope de Vega Carpio*, ed. Agustín Amezúa (Madrid, 1941), p. 324.

20. For a list of editions and translations of *Marcos de Obregón*, see the Bibliographical Note in *Vida del escudero Marcos de Obregón*, ed. María Soledad Carrasco Urgoiti (Madrid, 1972), I, 52–55.

21. Except where otherwise stated, this section is based upon the survey by Isabel Pope Conant, "Vicente Espinel as a Musician," in *Studies in the Renaissance*, V (1958), 133–44.

22. Quoted by Haley, *op. cit.*, p. 45.

23. Diego Vázquez Otero, *Vida de Vicente Martínez Espinel* (Málaga, 1948), p. 220.

24. See also Adolfo Salazar, "Música, instrumentos y danzas en las obras de Cervantes," *Nueva Revista de Filología Hispánica*, II (1948), 144–58, and A. Pardo Tovar, "Perfil y semblanza de Vicente Espinel," *Revista Musical Chilena*, XV (1961), 9–36 and XVI (1962), 6–30.

25. See T. Navarro Tomás, *Métrica española* (Madrid: Guadarrama, 1974), pp. 268–69.

26. For further reading on the subject of Espinel and the *décima*, see the articles by Dorothy Clotelle Clarke, José María de Cossío, Juan Millé y Giménez, and F. Sánchez y Escribano listed in the Selected Bibliography.

27. See *Diversas rimas, ed. cit.*, pp. 155–62 and, in particular, p. 161.

28. "Al Obispo de Málaga don Francisco Pacheco" in *Diversas rimas, ed. cit.*, pp. 73–74.

Chapter Two

1. This section is based upon the excellent survey of the poetic scene in Spain in the sixteenth and seventeenth centuries contained in the Introductions to Vols. I and II of A. Terry, *An Anthology of Spanish Poetry 1500–1700* (Oxford: Pergamon, 1965, 1968). The reader would also find useful R. O. Jones' chapters on sixteenth and seventeenth-century poetry in *A Literary History of Spain. The Golden Age: Prose and Poetry* (London: Benn, 1971), 90–120 and 141–66.

2. The circumstances surrounding the publication of *Diversas rimas* are more reliably reviewed in Haley, *op. cit.*, pp. 12–18, than in the Introduction to Dorothy Clotelle Clarke's edition of *Diversas rimas* which relies too heavily upon Juan Pérez de Guzmán.

3. The summary of Golden Age poetic practices in T. Navarro Tomás, *Métrica española* (Madrid: Guadarrama, 1974), pp. 251–304, has been valuable for this section, as was the more succinct Note on Versification in the two volumes of A. Terry, *Anthology*.

4. See T. Navarro Tomás, *op. cit.*, p. 284.

5. T. Navarro Tomás asserts (*op. cit.*, p. 268) that the strophe appears in "several of the compositions" in *Diversas rimas.*

6. For publication details of the "Sátira," see Chapter 1, note 6. It has not been studied in detail in the present work because of its relative inaccessibility. Chapter 1, Section XIII discusses the question of the *sonadas* and *cantares de sala* with which Espinel's name seems to have been associated. See also Isabel Pope Conant, *art. cit.*

7. See Chapter 1, Section VI and the extracts from contemporary documents reproduced by Haley, *op. cit.*, p. 25.

8. Interesting sidelights on the use of pseudonyms by Golden Age authors are shed by C. E. Anibal's study in his edition of Mira de Amescua, *El arpa de David* (Columbus, Ohio, 1925), pp. 124–90.

9. See Haley, *op. cit.*, p. 12.

10. Aspects of Espinel's poetic style are discussed in the Introduction to Dorothy Clotelle Clarke's edition of *Diversas rimas*, pp. 21–26 and more briefly in the Introduction to María Soledad Carrasco Urgoiti's edition of *Marcos de Obregón* I, 18–22.

Chapter Three

1. In this connection, the observations of Francisco Rico in *La novela picaresca y el punto de vista* (Barcelona: Seix Barral, 1970), pp. 108–14, are illuminating. See also: J. Cañedo, "El *curriculum vitae* del pícaro," *Revista de Filología Española*, XLIX (1966), 125–80; Claudio Guillén, "Towards a Definition of the Picaresque," in *Proceedings of the IIIrd Congress of the International Comparative Literature Association* (The Hague: Mouton & Co., 1962), pp. 252–66; A. A. Parker, *Literature and the Delinquent* (Edinburgh: University Press, 1967).

2. Alberto del Monte, *Itinerario de la novela picaresca española* (Barcelona: Lumen, 1971), pp. 58–61.

3. A. Zamora Vicente, "Tradición y originalidad en *El escudero Marcos de Obregón*" in *Presencia de los clásicos* (Buenos Aires, 1951), p. 83. Zamora Vincente, along with Alberto del Monte, *op. cit.*, pp. 108–109, and Marcel Bataillon, *Pícaros y picaresca* (Madrid, 1969), pp. 235–36, has insisted on the non-picaresque qualities of *Marcos de Obregón*.

4. See E. Nagy, "La honra y el marido agraviado en el *Marcos de Obregón*," *Hispania*, XLIII (1960), 541–44.

5. The section on the literary models of *Marcos de Obregón* in María Soledad Carrasco Urgoiti, *ed. cit.*, pp. 23–30, gives a brief survey of the novelistic scene at the time *Marcos* was written. Also useful in this connection is the corresponding section in Donald W. Bleznick, *Quevedo* (New York: Twayne, 1972), pp. 71–78. A more detailed review is to be found in R. O. Jones, *op. cit.*, pp. 50–74 and 122–40.

6. The Introduction by Jean Pierre Ressot to his edition (Madrid: Clásicos Castalia, 1972), pp. 30–34, deals with this point.

7. For a more detailed treatment of this aspect of *Marcos de Obregón* see Haley, *op. cit.*, pp. 65–82.

8. A. Rodríguez Moñino, in *Construcción crítica y realidad histórica en la poesía española de los siglos XVI y XVII* (Madrid, 1965), makes the point, for example, that many major Golden Age figures were virtually unknown to their contemporaries because their works were not printed in their lifetime.

9. See Juan Pérez de Guzmán, "Vicente Espinel y su obra" reprinted in *Vida de Marcos de Obregón* (Mexico: Editorial Porrúa, 1973), pp. xiii–xiv.

10. For a review of the circumstances surrounding this literary polemic, see Juan Pérez de Guzmán, *ed. cit.*, pp. xl–xlii.

11. Those interested in the *Gil Blas* affair will find bibliographical references in María Soledad Carrasco Urgoiti, *ed. cit.*, pp. 50–51.

12. Donald McGrady, *Mateo Alemán* (New York: Twayne, 1968), p. 54.

13. Especially useful in relation to this aspect of *Marcos de Obregón* is Haley, *op. cit.*, pp. 101–19. See also María Soledad Carrasco Urgoiti, *ed. cit.*, I, 31–36.

14. Concerning the interpretation of the word "descanso," see Ernest Muret, "Notes sur *Marcos de Obregón*" in *Mélanges de Linguistique et de Littérature offerts a M. Alfred Jeanroy* (Paris, 1928), pp. 325–32, and Samuel Gili Gaya, *ed. cit.*, I, 42, note 1.

15. For the confessional aspect of *Marcos de Obregón*, a useful parallel can be drawn with Diego de Torres Villarroel, *Vida, ascendencia, nacimiento, crianza y aventuras*. See the Introduction to the edition by Guy Mercadier (Madrid: Clásicos Castalia, 1972), especially pp. 21–33.

16. For an account of Espinel's work as a book censor for the Inquisition, see Haley, *op. cit.*, pp. 42–60.

17. A perceptive summary of Renaissance poetic theory is contained in the Introductions to Vols. I and II of A. Terry, *An Anthology*. See also Chapter 2, Section I of the present study.

18. For background material on the Aristotelian distinction between history and poetry, see Haley, *op. cit.*, pp. 83–100.

19. The section on the autobiographical elements in *Marcos de Obregón* in María Soledad Carrasco Urgoiti, *ed. cit.*, I, 36–41, provides an adequate summary of modern critical views.

20. References to Espinel's own division of the work into *relaciones* and *descansos* will be given thus in order to avoid confusion with textual references where the numbers cited allude to volume and page in the Gili Gaya edition.

21. For details of Espinel's circle of friends and acquaintances among the men of letters and influence at the time, see Zamora Vicente, *op. cit.*, 95–98, and Haley, *op. cit.*, 164–78.

22. See Jean-Jacques Rousseau, *Les Confessions*, VII, in *Oeuvres complètes* (Paris: Gallimard, 1959), I, 278. Related ideas on the nature of literary autobiography are discussed by Guy Mercadier, *ed. cit.*, pp. 31–33.

23. The examples of Unamuno, Gide, and Proust are cited by Haley, *op. cit.*, p. 66, 69, and 114, as illustrating the modern use of techniques experimented with by Espinel in *Marcos de Obregón*. See also the section below.

24. See E. Nagy, *art. cit.*

25. A brief survey of humor with reference to the picaresque novel in general and *Guzmán de Alfarache* in particular is to be found in Donald McGrady, *op. cit.*, pp. 71–74.

26. See Donald W. Bleznick, *op. cit.*, p. 84.

27. The document is reproduced in full as Appendix XXX in Haley, *op. cit.*, pp. 222–23.

28. Concerning digression in the picaresque novel, see: C. S. de Cortázar, "Notas para el estudio de la estructura del *Guzmán de Alfarache*," *Filología*, VII (1962), 79–95; Miguel Herrero, "Nueva interpretación de la novela picaresca," *Revista de Filología Española*, XXIV (1937), 343–62; Donald McGrady, *op. cit.*, pp. 74–79; F. Rico, *La novela picaresca es-*

pañola (Barcelona: Planeta, 1967), pp. cxiv–cxvii; Gonzalo Sobejano, "De la intención y valor del *Guzmán de Alfarache,*" *Romanische Forschungen,* LXXI (1959), 267–311.

29. Examination of a similar situation in *Guzmán de Alfarache* by Donald McGrady, *op. cit.*, pp. 145–67, offers an interesting comparison with *Marcos de Obregón.* See also the brief survey by María Soledad Carrasco Urgoiti, *ed. cit.*, I, 45–49.

30. Amos Parducci traces these borrowings in "Echi e Risonanze Boccaccesche nella *Vida de Marcos de Obregón,*" in *Mélanges de Linguistique et de Littérature Romanes offerts à Mario Roques* (Paris, 1953), II, pp. 207–17.

31. The Algiers sequence is studied in Haley, *op. cit.*, pp. 147–55.

32. See María Soledad Carrasco Urgoiti, *ed. cit.*, I, 47.

33. Marcos' encounter with Aurelio has been examined by Joseph Fucilla, "Sobre las fuentes de *Del rey abajo ninguno,*" in *Relaciones hispanoitalianas* (Madrid, 1953), pp. 191–93, Amos Parducci, *art. cit.*, pp. 211–12, and Giovanni Calabritto, *I Romanzi Picareschi di Mateo Alemán e Vicente Espinel* (Valletta, 1929), p. 156, note 17. The Camila sequence is also related to Italian sources by Calabritto, Parducci, and Caroline Bourland, "Boccaccio and the *Decameron* in Castilian and Catalan Literature," *Revue Hispanique,* XII (1905), 74–78.

34. Dr. Sagredo's adventures in the New World are the subject of Valentín de Pedro's "La 'geografía fantástica' de Vicente Espinel" in *América en las letras españolas del siglo de oro* (Buenos Aires: Editorial Sudamericana, 1954), pp. 112–32.

35. Zamora Vicente, *op. cit.*, p. 101. Espinel's prose style has been little studied. The lines of approach suggested by Zamora Vicente, see especially pp. 101–10, have formed the basis for this section. See also María Soledad Carrasco Urgoiti, *ed. cit.*, I, 49–50.

Chapter Four

1. For an examination of the circumstances surrounding the composition of the novel, see Haley, *op. cit.*, pp. 101–07.

2. The prefatory material is analyzed by Joseph L. Laurenti, "El prólogo en la novela picaresca española," in *Estudios sobre la novela picaresca española* (Madrid: C.S.I.C., 1970), pp. 3–22, and by Alberto Porqueras Mayo, *El prólogo en el manierismo y barroco españoles* (Madrid: C.S.I.C., 1968), pp. 12–13.

3. Details of the legend of the lovers of Antequera are given in Gili Gaya, *ed. cit.*, I, p. 37, note 8.

4. Amos Parducci, *art. cit.*, discusses the Italian sources of the opening sequence of chapters.

5. F. Rico, *op. cit.*, cix–cxii, offers interesting sidelights on the function of first-person narrative in the picaresque novel. See also: Carlos Blanco

Aguinaga, "Cervantes y la picaresca. Notas sobre dos tipos de realismo," *Nueva Revista de Filología Hispánica*, XI (1957), 131–42.

6. Haley, *op. cit.*, p. 169. reviews Espinel's association with the Church of San Andrés.

7. See Gili Gaya, *ed. cit.*, II, p. 221, note 6.

8. See E. Muret, *art. cit.*, p. 331.

9. Example quoted by Donald McGrady, *op. cit.*, p. 72.

10. Claudio Guillén, for instance, in reviewing Haley's book in *Romanic Review*, LII (1961), 56–59, believes that the latter has overworked the *Doppelgänger* effect by laying too much stress on this conventional formula.

11. For further clarification of this point, see: Haley, *op. cit.*, pp. 139–40; María Soledad Carrasco Urgoiti, *ed. cit.*, I, 121, note 213, and 305, note 1050.

12. Haley, *op. cit.*, pp. 151–55, indicates the extent of Espinel's borrowings from Luis de Mármol Carvajal and Diego de Haedo. See also Albert Mas, *Les Turcs dans la littérature espagnole du siècle d'or* (Paris: Centre de Recherches Hispaniques, 1967), I, 542–49. Guy Mercadier's review of Haley, *Bulletin Hispanique*, LXIV (1962), 88–92, supports the view that Espinel's sources are to be found in literature and descriptive geographies rather than in personal experience.

13. See María Soledad Carrasco Urgoiti, *ed. cit.*, II, 86, note 345.

14. The rejected *canción* and the three sonnets appear in Dorothy Clotelle Clarke, *ed. cit.*, pp. 149–52.

15. See Chapter 3, Section XI.

16. See: Valentín de Pedro, *art. cit.*, pp. 131–32; Gili Gaya, *ed. cit.*, II, 267, note 6, and 276, note 15; María Soledad Carrasco Urgoiti, *ed. cit.*, II, 240, note 1016; Haley, *op. cit.*, pp. 109–10.

Selected Bibliography

PRIMARY SOURCES

Diversas rimas. Madrid: Luis Sánchez, 1591. The only subsequent edition is that of Dorothy Clotelle Clarke, New York: Hispanic Institute, 1956. A reliable text, though it omits the translation of Horace, *Ars Poetica (Art of Poetry).*

Relaciones de la vida del escudero Marcos de Obregón (Account of the Life of the Squire Marcos de Obregón). Editions: Madrid: Juan de la Cuesta, 1618; illustrated edition prepared by Juan Pérez de Guzmán, Barcelona: Biblioteca Arte y Letras, 1881. The title appears here and subsequently as simply *Vida del escudero Marcos de Obregón.* The standard edition is by Samuel Gili y Gaya, Madrid: Clásicos Castellanos, 2 vols., 1922–25 (re-edited, with minor additions, 1951). María Soledad Carrasco Urgoiti, ed., *Vida del escudero Marcos de Obregón* Madrid: Clásicos Castalia, 2 vols., 1972. The only English translation is by Major Algernon Langton, London: John Booth, 2 vols., 1816.

"Sátira contra las damas de Sevilla." Reproduced by Eugenio Mele and Adolfo Bonilla y San Martín, *Revista de Archivos, Bibliotecas y Museos,* X (1904), 410–15.

Translation of Horace, *Ars Poetica.* Originally published as part of *Diversas rimas.* Reproduced by López de Sedano in *Parnaso Español,* I, Madrid: Ibarra, 1768.

SECONDARY SOURCES

1. *Biography*

ENTRAMBASAGUAS, JOAQUÍN DE. "Datos biográficos de Vicente Espinel en sus *Diversas rimas*," *Revista Bibliográfica y Documental,* IV (1950), 171–241. Attempt to use the poems as a source of biographical information. Needs to be read in the light of Haley (see below).

_____. "Vicente Espinel, poeta de la reina Ana de Austria," *Revista de Literatura,* VIII (1955), 228–38; IX (1956) 139–48. Summary of information on Espinel's poetic activities in Italy.

155

HALEY, GEORGE. *Vicente Espinel and* Marcos de Obregón. *A Life and Its Literary Representation.* Providence, Rhode Island: Brown University Press, 1959. Fundamental documentary study of the life of Espinel; strips away the inherited errors which had arisen from an uncritical reliance on data supplied by the poems and the novel.

VÁZQUEZ OTERO, DIEGO. *Vida de Vicente Martínez de Espinel.* Málaga: Diputación Provincial, 1948. Readable but romanticized biography, places too much faith in uncorroborated statements in *Marcos de Obregón.*

2. *Bibliography*

LAURENTI, JOSEPH P. *Ensayo de una bibliografía de la novela picaresca (1554-1964).* Madrid: C.S.I.C., 1968. Valuable list of editions, translations, monographs, and articles.

SERÍS, HOMERO. *Nuevo ensayo de una biblioteca española de libros raros y curiosos,* I, New York: Hispanic Society of America, 1969, pp. 344-56. Best survey of editions and bibliographical studies; also includes critical works on Espinel.

SIMÓN-DÍAZ, JOSÉ. *Bibliografía de la literatura hispánica,* IX, Madrid: C.S.I.C., 1971, pp. 676-88. Supplements Laurenti.

Espinel as Musician

CONANT, ISABEL POPE. "Vicente Espinel as a Musician," *Studies in the Renaissance,* V (1958), 133-44. Biographical information based on Pérez de Guzmán; helpful review of Espinel's contribution to the rise of the guitar.

PARDO TOVAR, A. "Perfil y semblanza de Vicente Espinel," *Revista Musical Chilena,* XV (1961), 9-36; XVI (1962), 6-30. Interesting on the links between popular music and polyphony from sixteenth century; relates Espinel's musical ideas to those of his contemporaries.

3. *Espinel as Poet*

CLARK, DOROTHY CLOTELLE. "Sobre la espinela," *Revista de Filología Española,* XXIII (1936), 293-304. Survey of evidence in favor of Espinel's invention of the verse-form which bears his name.

———. "A note on the *décima* or *espinela*," *Hispanic Review,* VI (1938), 155-58. Rebuttal of Millé y Giménez.

COSSÍO, JOSÉ MARÍA DE. "La décima antes de Espinel," *Revista de Filología Española,* XXVIII (1944), 428-54. Synopsis of experiments toward *espinela;* stresses Lope de Vega's part in associating the name of Espinel with the strophe.

MILLÉ Y GIMÉNEZ, JUAN. "Sobre la invención de la décima o espinela," *Hispanic Review,* VI (1937), 40-51. Plays down Espinel's role by pointing to earlier experiments.

SÁNCHEZ Y ESCRIBANO, F. "Un ejemplo de la espinela anterior a 1571," *Hispanic Review*, VIII (1940) 349–51. Produces an early example of the form by Juan de Mal Lara.

Espinel as Novelist

CALABRITTO, GIOVANNI. *I romanzi picareschi di Mateo Alemán e Vicente Espinel*. Valetta Tip. del Malta, 1929. An early study, chiefly useful for indicating the Italian sources of some episodes.

FABBIANI RUIZ, J. "El paisaje en Espinel y el áspero humorismo de Quevedo" in *Clásicos castellanos (Novelas y novelistas)*. Caracas: Elite, 1944. Draws attention to Espinel's natural descriptions.

FUCILLA, JOSEPH. "Sobre las fuentes de *Del rey abajo ninguno*" in *Relaciones hispanoitalianas*. Madrid: Anejos de la Revista de Filología Española, 1953. Ariosto, Espinel, and Rojas Zorrilla.

HALEY, GEORGE. *Vicente Espinel and Marcos de Obregón. A Life and Its Literary Representation*. Providence, Rhode Island: Brown University Press, 1959. Deserves a double mention because the second half of the book is devoted to a study of Marcos as Espinel's *alter ego*, of the combination of fact and fiction in the work, and of the interplay between the time-levels represented. Sometimes over-subtle, but a masterly analysis.

MONTE, ALBERTO DEL. *Itinerario del romanzo picaresco spagnolo*. Florence: Sansoni, 1957. Spanish translation, Barcelona: Lumen, 1971. Excellent survey of the picaresque novel with a useful summary of work done on *Marcos de Obregón* and good bibliographical references.

NAGY, EDWARD. "La honra y el marido agraviado en el *Marcos de Obregón* de Vicente Espinel," *Hispania*, XLIII (1960), 541–44. Aurelio episode taken as evidence of a more humane attitude toward honor.

PARDUCCI, AMOS. "Echi e risonanze boccaccesche nella *Vida de Marcos de Obregón*," in *Mélanges de Linguistique et de Littérature Romanes offerts à Mario Roques*, II, Paris: Droz, 1953, pp. 207–17. Traces of the Decameron found in various episodes of *Marcos de Obregón*.

ZAMORA VICENTE, ALONSO. "Tradición y originalidad en el *Escudero Marcos de Obregón*" in *Presencia de los clásicos*. Buenos Aires: Espasa-Calpe, 1951, pp. 75–140. Wide-ranging, impressionistic criticism but with the right insights, particularly about the non-picaresque nature of the work, the feeling for landscape, and Espinel's use of language.

Index

158

Pérez Roy, Francisco, 91
Petrarch, 38, 67
Philip II, 33, 117, 129, 131, 141
Philip III, 22, 103, 143
Philosophia antigua poetica. See López
  Pinciano, Alonso
Phyllis, 20, 52
Pícara Justina, La. See López de Ubeda,
  Francisco
Pícaro, 61–62, 87, 89–91, 98, 107, 113,
  120, 137
Pigafetta, Antonio, 141
Pindar, 41
Pirandello, Luigi, 110
Po, river, 130, 132
Poema trágico del Español Gerardo. See
  Céspedes y Meneses, Gonzalo de
Ponces de Barcelona, Los. See Vega
  Carpio, Lope Félix de
Pontedeume, 137
Porqueras Mayo, Alberto, 152n2
Premio de la constancia, El. See Espinel
  Adorno, Jacinto de
Proust, Marcel, 110, 151n23; *A la re-
  cherche du temps perdu,* 85, 138
Puente de Segovia, 109–10, 121
Pujol, Luis, 67

"¿Qué me queda que esperar?," 56
Quevedo y Villegas, Francisco de, 13,
  21, 26, 32, 36, 40, 42, 45, 52, 62, 65,
  86, 90, 112, 136; *Buscón, El,* 23, 61,
  91, 107, 114, 137
Quiñones, Vigil de, 115

Reconquest, 14, 81
"Redondillas a una lima," 43
Rennert, Hugo A., 148n13
Repullés, Mateo, 111
Ressot, Jean Pierre, 150n6
Rico, Francisco, 150n1, 151n28, 152n5
Rio de Janeiro, 141
Rioja, Francisco de, 49
Riselo, 48
Rodríguez Marín, Francisco, 147n7
Rodríguez Moñino, Antonio, 150n8
Rojas, Agustín de: *Viaje entretenido, El,*
  65

Rojas Zorrilla, Francisco de, 157; *Del rey
  abajo, ninguno,* 133
Romancero General, 21
Ronda, 14–16, 18–23, 25, 29, 33–34, 39,
  40, 45, 47–48, 52–53, 70–71, 73,
  79–81, 83–84, 88–89, 101, 108, 110,
  112–14, 116–19, 121, 130, 135, 137,
  139, 140–41
Rousseau, Jean-Jacques, 81, 151n22
Rueda, Lope de, 132
Ruiz de Alarcón, Juan, 30

Sacchetti, Franco, 132
Sagredo, Dr., 63–64, 70–72, 84, 88, 92,
  96–99, 102, 106–108, 110–11, 125,
  128, 134, 136–37, 140–42, 152n34
Saint Isidore, 23, 29
Saint Teresa, 23
Salamanca, 15–16, 28, 35, 70, 79, 83,
  90–91, 110, 114–17
Salamanca, University of, 14–15, 79
Salas Barbadillo, Alonso Jerónimo de,
  21, 26
Salazar, Adolfo, 148n24
Salinas, Francisco de, 15, 115
San Andrés, Church of, 20, 26–27, 29,
  81, 108, 112, 153n6
San Bernardo, Abbot of, 66
Sánchez, José, 148n13
Sánchez, Luis, 155
Sánchez y Escribano, F., 149n26, 157
Sancho Panza, 89, 115
Sandoval y Rojas, Bernardo de, Cardinal
  Archbishop of Toledo, 14, 26, 85,
  105–106, 112
San Ginés, tomb of, 80, 102
San Juan de la Cruz, 36
Sanlúcar, 125–26, 141
San Pedro, Diego de: *Cárcel de amor,*
  59, 67
San Pelayo, Colegio Mayor de, 16,
  115–16
San Pier d'Arena, 130
Santa Bárbara, Hospital Real de, 18–19
Santa Catalina de los Donados, 63, 69,
  73, 107, 129, 143
Santa Cruz, Melchor de: *Floresta es-
  pañola de apotegmas y sentencias,* 65
Santa María la Mayor, Church of, 19